First Published on Amazon Kind
2021.

Cover Photography by Martin Fairhurst.

Pentacle Illustration by Sye Watts.

Book Website: www.spellcastbook.com

Antony Simpson's Blog: www.antonysimpson.com

The use of essential oils recommended in this book are for use on **adults only**.

We also recommend doing a skin test with a small amount to check for any allergic reaction. In the event of an allergic reaction wash off the oil and any herbs used immediately.

Any allergic reaction can be **life threatening** and you should **call your emergency services in the event of having a serious adverse reaction to any oil, herb or plant.**

Contents   Pages 3-6

Forward   Pages 7-9

Spells
Instant Magic   Pages 10-14

Banishment & Bindings   Pages 15-24

Blessings   Pages 25-31

Cleansing   Pages 32-38

Forward

A Druid and a Witch got together and decided to write a book. They wanted something fresh and different to what was already out there. They wanted a practical magic spell book that didn't include the basics (such as how to cast a circle, how spells work, etc.) and that didn't include any religion or ethics. This is how SpellCast was born.

This book has been designed for intermediate to advanced magical practitioners. It has tried and tested spells that work; with some that will stand the test of time. The spells are organised into categories for ease. The magic is essentially folk magic.

We have used magic in many different ways, including: in baths, candles, chants, charms, colour, cords, crystals, elemental magic, calling upon Gods & Goddesses, magic squares, nature magic, oils, incense, planet and star magic, ritual, talismans, poppets, Ogham script, witch bottles, and visualisation.

We have designed each Spell to deal with 21st century problems and done our best to make sure that all ingredients are easily available. In the event that you can't get hold of an ingredient, check the last page of the chapter for a table of correspondents that will list suitable substitutes.

We hope you find this book fun, informative and above all effective in achieving your desired results.

Brightest Blessings,

Luna Hare & Antony Simpson
2020

About Us
Luna Hare is in his 50s and has been a practicing pagan since his late 20s, but he has always had magic in his life. He was initiated into a coven in the early days of him coming out as a witch and is still in contact with the original group. After learning his craft with the group, he found the rigidity of the Wiccan path too restricting so looked for other alternatives. It was here he came across Druidry and joined the OBOD (Order of Bards, Ovates and Druids) where his creativity and free spirit felt more at home.

Luna has since become a more spiritual and grounded pagan and feels that too much focus on the religion is not always necessary. Luna now classes himself as a Wise Man with knowledge of many of the different aspects of paganism. Luna specialises in crystals, aromatherapy, healing, rituals, blessings, fertility, poppets, poetry, talismans, charms and nature magic.

Antony Simpson is a Witch who has been an eclectic pagan for over 18 years. He has worked as both a solitary practitioner and in groups. Antony is good at instant magic and being the darker practitioner of the two, naturally leans towards banishments & bindings, spells around material gain, healing and protection.

Types of magic that Antony specialises in include: candle magic, chants, charms, colour, crystals, elemental magic, invocation of gods and goddesses, nature magic, oils, rituals, visualisation and witch bottles.

Instant Magic

For quick, instant, results. For when there is no time like the present for manifestation. These spells require no preparation and are effective whenever they are cast. As such there are no correspondences for these spells.

Car Parking Space Chant
When it is difficult to find a car parking space, repeat this chant until you find a space, which will be soon:

Powers of Earth, Sea and Sky,
Find me a parking space that's close by.

Lost Items Chant
Repeat this chant until you find your lost item:

I call upon the spirits of things that disappear.
[name of object] I wish to find,
So help me now out of this bind.
So must it be.

Be sure to thank the spirits when you find your lost item. Say something like:

Spirits I thank thee for your time, with this simple little rhyme.

To Slow Time

Running late? Look at a clock or watch and visualise the second hand move slower and slower, ticking by much slower than usual. Then say:

Janus, keeper of time, here my plea,
Slow time until I get to where I need to be.

Or if you need more time to get something done, use the same visualisation but adapt the words. Say:

Janus, keeper of time, here my plea,
Slow time until my task completed be.

Mirrored Psychic Protection Bubble

If you ever find yourself under psychic attack, close your eyes and visualise a protection bubble. On the outside visualise the surface of your protection bubble as mirrored. A reflective surface deflecting negative energy back to its sender. You'll find that the attack soon stops.

If it doesn't strengthen the protection bubble with energy from the universe; visualise a beam of energy coming down from the stars and strengthening your psychic protection bubble making it strong and impenetrable.

It might be worth revisiting your self-protection. See the

Protection chapter of this book.

Physical Protection Bubble

The best way to avoid harm is to prevent it. This exercise should be undertaken daily, so that when you need it the most, you're able to throw up a good protective bubble.

This physical protection bubble is to be used as a last resort. The time to use it, is in the moments when time slows right before an accident or incident and nothing else can be done.

For example, Antony once used this when a car came round a blind corner at 40 MPH and Antony was crossing the road. Time slowed. Antony wasn't going to make it out of the way of the on-coming car. The driver hadn't even seen Antony yet. The driver was speeding and not paying attention.

Antony used this protection bubble, casting it outside of his aura and the car hit it. The car was slowed by the impact and the driver then noticed Antony and slammed hard on his breaks. All this time Antony kept moving and he managed to be just inches over to the other side of the road, so that the car just missed him. Antony would probably be dead if it wasn't for the few seconds of time his physical protection bubble had bought him.

This visualisation is a simple one. Imagine a bubble of green energy, strong and impenetrable around you. Make it thick and put the bubble outside of your aura, which can be several feet away from your body.

Everyday add more energy to this bubble through repeating the visualisation. Be confident in knowing that when you need it, you'll be able to call upon the bubble of physical protection.

Energy Balls
Place your first two fingers of both hands facing one another a couple of inches apart. Visualise energy flowing between them making a sphere that slowly increases in size. As this energy flows and builds give it a purpose with your mind. Visualise the energy ball setting to work and the task being complete. When you feel that enough energy has been raised you can release the energy ball or throw it (depending on your intention) and it will go to work instantly. This is great for any sort of Spell involving technology.

For example, a slow computer, tablet or smart phone can be sped up by charging an energy ball and then releasing it onto and into the computer.

To Keep Warm in Cold Weather
Run your hands together until they are warm. Visualise yourself being stood in a red walled protection bubble with the red walls being that of flames. Bring this bubble in close to your physical body. Feel the heat on any exposed skin, I.e., hands, face. Etc. Say these words of power:

Powers of fire and flame,
Make me hot, this is my aim.
As hot as the sun on a summer's day,
Do this now without delay.

The reverse can be done if you feel too hot. Visualise yourself being stood in a yellow walled protection bubble with the yellow walls being walls of cool air. Bring this bubble in close to your physical body. Feel the cool air on your exposed skin, hands, arms, face, etc. Say these words of power:

Powers of air around me,
Cool me down I ask thee.
As cool as a fresh breeze on an autumn's day,
Do this now without delay.

To Make a Computer, Tablet or Smartphone Run Quicker

1. Restart your computer or device and as it reboots say:

Powers of Earth, Sea, Wind & Sky,
Make this device quick and fly.
Not a moment of wasted time there shall be,
Let this device be all that it should be.
So mote it be.

Banishment & Bindings

GET MAD

Sometimes we can get stuck,

Feeling like we have no luck.

Forgetting the power within,

To change things so that we can win.

Not all that others perceive as bad is bad,

Sometimes it does good to get more than a little mad.

To rage, be angry, be frustrated and annoyed,

To take action rather than to avoid.

To cast a defensive Spell or two,

In order to protect you.

Remember that emotion is key,

For true any Spell to be.

A Note on HEXs & Curses

We don't generally as a rule recommend that you HEX or Curse someone. This rule comes from our own experience. It takes a lot of energy to throw a good HEX or Curse and while it's totally doable and works, they never seem to resolve anything. Knowing everything is going wrong in an enemy's life is great, but apart from that they're still going to cause you hassle. So much better to bind then, or even better banish them completely from your life.

Not all bindings or banishments are bad. Antony once cast a banishing spell for a bad boss he had. The boss had made Antony's life a nightmare. Antony banished the boss and the boss left to a job that was better paid, better working conditions and better suited to them. It was a win-win for both Antony and the bad boss.

The Almost Famous Freezer Bag Spell

Sometimes in life people need to literally chill out. Your boss giving you a hard time at work? A family member being difficult? Then this is the perfect Spell. For this spell you will need:

- A piece of paper.
- A pen.
- A freezer bag.

1. Write the person's full name on a piece of paper, preferably in black ink.

2. Fold and put in a freezer bag.

3. Then fill the bag with water until the slip of paper is covered.

4. Place in the bottom draw of your freezer.

This spell can be easily reversed, by simply taking the bag out of the freezer and allowing it to defrost. Just be careful not to defrost it too soon, otherwise you'll be putting them back into the freezer again.

Bye, Bye Boat Banishment

This spell is good for banishing someone's issues. For this spell you will need:

- A piece of paper.
- A pen with black ink.
- Vetiver essential oil.

1. Make a boat out of the piece of paper. A YouTube search will help you learn how to make one easily. Write the name of the person whose issues you wish to banish and their birthday on the boat.

2. Anoint the boat with three drops of Vetiver.

3. Take the boat to a fresh stream. Place the boat in the water and say (as the boat floats away):

Stop this person being unkind,
To this craft his/her issues bind.

Take then far, so far away,
Bring kindness and love instead today.

Banishing A Person Spell
This Spell is to completely banish a person out of your life for good. It should be used with caution as may bring unforeseen changes to your life. For this spell you will need:

- A black candle.
- Something to scratch the candle.
- X6 drops of Cinnamon essential oil.
- X6 drops of Patchouli essential oil.

1. Charge the black candle by visualising the person you wish to banish leaving your life.

2. Scratch the initials of the person you wish to banish on the black candle. Anoint the candle.

3. Cast a circle. Then say these words as you light the candle:

Powers of the universe hear my plea,
Come forth and surround thee.
Aid me in this spell,
And do so well.

Get out, Get out, Get out!
That's what this spell is all-about.

[full name] leave my life for good,

Do this now you should.

Get out, Get out, Get out!
That's what this spell is all-about.

Don't hesitate or delay,
There is no time like today.

Get out, Get out, Get out!
That's what this spell is all-about.

So leave now, be gone, I command,
Get out of my life, for you are now banned.

As I will it, so it is.

4. Allow the candle to burn down fully, then throw the remains in the bin outside.

The Ultimate Binding Person Spell

This binding binds the person from being unkind, mean and helps people see the person for how they truly are. For this spell you will need:

- A piece of paper.
- A black pen.
- A black charm bag.
- Black Tourmaline or Black Onyx Crystal.
- Smokey Quartz Crystal.
- Cinnamon Herb or Cinnamon essential oil.
- Vetiver essential oil.
- Sage essential oil.

1. Take the paper and pen and write as much about the person as you can. Their name, birthday, where they live, etc. Even better if you can get a tag lock (some hair or nail clippings) add those too. Fold this paper up and place it in the charm bag.

2. Put the following into the charm bag:

- A pinch of Cinnamon or x3 drops of Cinnamon essential oil.

- X2 drops of Vetiver essential oil.
- X1 drop of Sage essential oil.

3. Take the crystals and charge them with your intention. Charge the Smokey Quartz to block the negative energies from the person. Charge the Black Tourmaline or Black Onyx to control the person like a puppet on a string and control their bad behaviour.

4. Now close the charm bag and say over it three times:

I bind you and your wicked ways,
From now and for all future days.

Let you be no longer mean, critical or cruel.
Let you treat me with respect and no longer like a fool.

By the powers that be,
I charge these crystals to set me free.
Free from your bullshit and lies,
Now everyone will see through your nice disguise.
Everyone will see you for what you truly are,
A fraud, a fake, anything but a star.

I bind you and your wicked ways,
From now and for all future days.

5. Carry the charm bag with you in future dealings with this person. You'll see a dramatic change in how they treat you and in how they are perceived by others.

Get Rid of Bad Habits Spell

This Spell is a great way to get rid of a bad habit. For this spell you will need:

- Toilet roll.
- Marker Pen.
- Toilet.

1. Take a piece of toilet roll paper and the marker pen. Write down any bad habits that you want to get rid of on the toilet paper. After you have written them down, cross them out and then put a large **X** over the crossings out.

2. Go to the toilet and wipe yourself using the toilet paper. Wipe forwards (urine) for minor bad habits or backwards (faeces) for more stubborn bad habits.

3. Then flush away the toilet paper and say goodbye to those bad habits.

This spell can also be adapted to work on others. Simply write their full name at the top of the toilet paper, don't cross out the name or have the **X** covering the name. Flush away without wiping. Under **no circumstances** cross out the person's name or put the X over the person's name or both, as this may lead to unintended negative consequences.

To Banish Annoying Attitudes and Attributes in Others

Tired of another's traits or attitudes? Banish them using this Spell. For this spell you will need:

- Two pieces of paper and a pen.
- A black candle.
- Some black ribbon.
- A fire proof dish.

1. Take a piece of paper and write the full name of a person whose annoying attitudes and attributes you wish to banish. If you can get hold of their date of birth, add that too. Then list all the attitudes and attributes you wish to banish.

2. Light the candle and say three times:

Power of fire, burn and glow,
Banish [name of person]'s traits into the cosmos so.

3. Set light to the piece of paper using the black candle and allow to fully burn to ashes in the fire proof dish.

4. Next take the other piece of paper. Write down the full name of the person and date of birth if known. Write down how you would like he or she to treat you. Be as detailed as possible with this. Take the ribbon and tie around the paper and say this as you do three times:

Tied you are and bound you be,
Until you transform and do this to me.

5. Keep the paper safe and don't untie until you wish to release the person.

Banishment & Bindings Correspondences

Colours	Crystals
• Black • Dark Purple • Dark Blue	• Obsidian (Black) • Haematite • Smokey Quartz • Jet (Black)
Days of the Week	**Elements**
• Tuesday • Thursday • Saturday	• Earth • Fire
Essential Oils	**Phase(s) of The Moon**
• Cinnamon • Myrrh • Patchouli • Vetiver • Sage • Sandalwood	• Full Moon • Waning
Herbs, Trees & Plants	**Planets**
• Plants: Rose, Cactus. • Trees: Hawthorn, Willow. • Herbs: Cinnamon, Fenell.	• Mars • Earth

Blessings

NATURE'S BLESSING

As I stand beneath the spreading leaves of nature's warm embrace,

I give thanks to the spirits and the powers of this place.

Let magic flow from deep within and carry words of peace,

As above so below to north, south, west and east.

I pray that every single soul can hear that they are loved,

I pray the Lord and Lady can here me up above.

No matter our religion there's no more need to fight,

Our colour makes no difference for we all need sleep at night.

Take lessons from the forest unite and live as one,

For our future holds one certainty when the world is gone it's gone...

A Blessing for Every Occasion

This chapter contains blessings for every occasion. A blessing is an special act, one where words are spoken aloud to bestow positive energies on a person or place.

New Baby Blessing

Mother goddess bless this child.
Grant [him/her] future joy.
Mother goddess keep [him/her] safe.
With the magic you employ,
Give Earth a strong foundation.
On which [he/she] can grow.
Give Air to aid with clarity,
As winds of time will blow.
Give Fire for power and passion,
For a future filled with love.
Give Water to inspire [his/her] dreams.
With guidance from above,
Last of all give Spirit.
So this child can truly shine.
[We/I] thank you Mother goddess,
For your blessings and your time.

Birthday Blessing

Today we celebrate your birth.
A magical event,
Created by two people's love.
From the heavens you were sent.
Each passing year builds a tale,
Like bricks within a wall,
And tells the story of your life.
Since you were very small,
As the wall grows bigger,
A mural will unfold,
A multitude of colours,
For the whole world to behold.
So take your birthday candles,
And make a magic wish with wonder,
Blow the spell and set it free,
For the universe to ponder.
Enjoy the hours of this your day.
For they are yours to spend,
Best wishes for the future.
Bright blessings my dear friend.

HandFasting Blessing

As you come together to join as one,
take joy in what there is to come.
May your future hold a blessing,
mother moon and father sun.
Each day will be an adventure,
for you to meet with pride.
Each night will be a chance to hold,
Your lover by your side.
This union is sacred,
You were bound for all to see.
To share not only this life,
But through all eternity.
Be kind to one another,
Hold dear your sacred vow.
Your future holds a mystery,
And the mystery starts now.

Anniversary Blessing

With every circle of the year we mark the paths of time,
Today brings yet another mark upon the futures line.
A year of love and sharing, a period of growth,
A time to reflect on what's been since you took your oath.
Give thanks for all the little things be grateful for each
other.
Give blessings for another year the ground that you have
covered.

Let go of disagreements, banish thoughts of pain,
Remember you come this far and long may you remain.
Be open to the future and long may you understand,
that a path that's shared together passes quickly hand in
hand.

Elemental Relationship Blessing

I invoke the elements on this [month] day,
let them give their blessing on our relationship in every
possible way.
Hail to the Watchtowers of the North,
Powers of Mother Earth,
Bless this relationship with Strength and Trust.
Thanks to Mother Earth.
Hail to the Watchtowers of the East,
Powers of Wind and Air,
Bless this relationship with intellect, creativity and
inspiration.
Thanks to the element of air.
Hail to the Watchtowers of the South,
Powers of the Sun and Fire,
Bless this relationship with lust, love and passion.
Thanks to the flame.
Hail to the Watchtowers of the West,
Powers of Emotion and Water,
Bless this relationship with honest, clear, communication.
Thanks to the lakes and oceans.

Friendship Blessing

I am lucky beyond reckoning
to have you as a friend.
Your energy and attitude,
is such a perfect blend.
Your always there to catch me,
if I stumble or I fall,
whenever I am feeling low,
you know just when to call.
The times we share are filled with love.
I'm thankful for our time.
There's joy in every step we take.
You truly help me shine.
I ask the Sun and Moon and Stars,
To watch over all you do.
And I thank the Lord and Lady,
For the blessing that is YOU....

Health Blessing

Lord and Lady of the Sun and Moon,
Send Blessings to me now.
Heal my body and my soul.
Let nature's rhythms flow.
Fill me with your energies.
Bless me with your power.
Keep me healthy here and now,

and every future hour.

Funeral Blessing

At this time of heartfelt sorrow.
As we celebrate your life.
We remember all the times we shared.
That made our time so bright.
The Shadowlands are waiting,
so set your spirit free.
And dance among the moon and stars.
Until your time to leave.
Each life is but a circle,
no beginning and no end.
This is just another journey,
for your soul to comprehend.
Fly swiftly through the afterlife,
Take heed in what you've learned.
The next life will be filled with joy.
As the circle starts to turn,
we miss you and we understand,
Your time with us must end.
Take blessings from this life you lived,
and start to live again...

Cleansing

GIVE THANKS

I Know that every raindrop,

Holds a blessing from the sky.

I know that every snowflake,

Falls from an Angel's eye.

I listen for the ancestors,

In the valley of the hills.

I see reflections of the Lady,

In the waters that lie still.

Feel the words of the water sprites,

As rivers and streams flow by.

Hear the call of the ancient warrior,

In the lonesome buzzard's cry.

I Sense the power of magic.

Atop the mountain's white,

I wait to learn the mysteries,

In the dead of dark moon nights.

I long to dance between the stars.

Trade kisses with my dreams.

Give thanks to the Lord and Lady,

For helping me to see these things.

Aura Cleanse

This is the ultimate self-cleanse. This can be done in the shower or bathtub.

1. Remove all jewelry and clothing and physically clean yourself from head to toe.

2. Next imagine energy from the universe as a bright white light flowing over you and within you. Feel the energy penetrate your hair, skin and muscles through to your bones.

At each Chakra feel the energy flow into the vortex and restore it to its rightful colour.

3. Once you have completed each Chakra, feel the energy extend to the outer edges of your Aura and visualise the outer edge encompassed in the universal energy.

4. Next visualise roots from your feet travelling down into the depths of the earth and feel any excess energy release into the earth.

This whole process should take about 20 minutes.

Home Cleanse

Cleanse your home using this Spell. You can also add protection in at the same time by using the Powerful Protection Incense in the Protection Chapter of this book. For this you will need:

- Incense or a sage stick.
- A drum or bell.

1. Open all windows and doors where possible.

2. Starting from the front door walking anti clockwise around every room waft the incense into every corner and drum or ring the bell in every corner. When you have been through every room and you return to the front door push all the negative energy outside and close the door and say:

Be gone all negativity let only positivity rest here.

3. Leave incense to burn down and close windows and doors.

Work Cleanse
It can be more difficult to cleanse work environments due to other people's energy. However, you can cleanse your own private workspace or shared meeting rooms through visualisation.

To do this visualise a bright white light shine down from the universe and cleanse the space of all negativity. Be aware that this might take longer than a usual cleansing, as other people's negative residue can be quite difficult to banish.

Altar & Ritual Tools Cleanse

It is a good idea to cleanse your altar and ritual tools before their first use and on a regular basis. For this you will need:

- Water.
- Salt.
- Incense.
- X1 White candle.

1. Cast your circle in the usual way.

2. Kneel or stand before the altar and add salt to the water and sprinkle the altar with the salted water. Ask the universe or deity of your choice to cleanse the working area.

3. Taking your magical tools one at a time, sprinkle each with the salted water, pass through the flame of the candle and then through the smoke of the incense. Visualise all the energy of each item being filled with the powers of the elements.

4. Rest the cleansed items on a cloth or pentacle until the circle is closed.

Cleansing Oil Mix

Here is a good cleansing oil mix we developed after much experimentation:

- 5mls of Base oil.
- X3 drops of Myrrh essential oil.
- X2 drops of Sage essential oil.
- X2 drops of Lavender essential oil.
- X3 drops of Rosemary essential oil.

Cleansing Correspondences

Colours	Crystals
• White • Pale Blue • Pale Pink	• Amethyst • Clear Quartz • Selenite • Blue Calcite • Celestite • Lapis Lazuli
Days of the Week	**Elements**
• Sunday • Monday • Saturday	• Air • Water
Essential Oils	**Phase(s) of The Moon**
• Sage • Lavender • Grapefruit • Rosemary • Myrrh • Chamomile • Mugwort	• Any • Even better if you can work in sunlight.
Herbs, Trees & Plants	**Planets**
• Plants: Sage. • Trees: Pine. • Herbs: Sage, Rosemary & Eucalyptus.	• The Sun • Saturn

Communication

LISTEN

Listen to the Earth and hear her beating heart,

Listen to the mountains here from the start.

Listen to the oceans deep and wide and blue,

Listen to the forest that works so hard for you.

Tell the world your grateful for all her many wonders.

Tell the mountains too as you sit among the thunder.

Tell the mighty ocean all your hopes and fears.

Hold the mighty oak tree that has stood for many years.

Converse with all the creatures that can help you become whole,

Speak freely and from the heart and listen to your soul.

Give thanks for all the joyfulness that nature has to give,

Communicate and listen well, the don't be afraid to live.

To Aid Better Communication

Want to communicate better? To be clear and concise and for others to understand exactly what you're saying? Then this is the perfect Spell for you. For this spell you will need:

- A Blue candle.
- A White candle.
- A Knife.
- Lemongrass essential oil.

1. Charge the candles with your intention. Charge the white candle for clarity. Charge the blue candle visualising calm talking and active listening.

2. Use the knife to mark the symbol for Mercury on the blue candle. The symbol for Mercury is as follows:

3. Use the knife to mark the following rune on the white candle:

4. Anoint both candles with Lemongrass essential oil.

5. Separate the two candles so that they are approximately 9 inches apart.

6. Each day light the candles for 1 hour, move them an inch closer and say:

Mercury please hear me.
Come and give your aid.
Help me to communicate,
And find the words to say.
Mercury give me answers.
Make my thinking clear.
Help me find the right words,
So my voice all will hear.

7. Repeat step 6 each day until both candles have fully burned down.

To Speak Confidently and Clearly Charm

Not a fan of public speaking? This Spell will help. For this spell you will need:

- A blue charm bag.
- X3 small Lapis Lazuli crystals.
- X1 larger Clear Quartz crystal.
- Lavender (fresh).
- Lavender (seed).
- Mint leaves (fresh).
- Frankincense essential oil.

- Lemongrass essential oil.
- Geranium essential oil.
- Base oil.
- An empty essential oils bottle, ideally one with a pipette.

1. Make up the oil and pour into the empty essential oil bottle:

- X9 drops of Frankincense.
- X4 drops of Lemongrass.
- X3 drops of Geranium.
- 5-10mls of base oil.

2. Place the following into the charm bag:

- The crystals.
- Mint leaves.
- Lavender (both fresh and seed).

3. Drop x6 drops of the oil into the charm bag and say:

I add life to this charm bag every day,
Help me speak clearly in every possible way,

4. Each day 'feed' your bag a drop of the oil mix and repeat:

I add life to this charm bag every day,

Help me speak clearly in every possible way.

To Be Heard Incantation

Say this incantation to be heard by others:

Mercury let my voice be heard,
Let everyone hear every single word.
I have so much to say,
So now is the time today.
For me to speak up, my voice clear,
To an open mind and listening ear.
Let all my body language convey,
The things that I wish to say.
Let my written words do the same,
Any overwriting be tame.
As I will it, so it is.

Contact Me Now Spell

Want someone to call, text or message you? Then this Spell is for you. For this spell you will need:

- A green piece of paper and a pen.
- Sellotape.

1. Write the name of the person you want to contact you on the piece of paper and sellotape it to the back of your

phone or phone case.

2. Then say:

[Name] contact me now.
I want to hear your voice,
Or maybe just a message,
You really have no choice.

Communication Correspondences

Colours	Crystals
• Light Blue • Lavender	• Lapis Lazuli • Aquamarine • Haematite • Apatite • Chalcedony • Chrysocolla • Fluorite
Days of the Week • Wednesday • Sunday • Thursday	**Elements** • Air • Water
Essential Oils • Lemongrass • Peppermint • Lavender • Frankincense • Geranium • Jasmine • Cypress	**Phase(s) of The Moon** • New Moon
Herbs, Trees & Plants • Plants: Vanilla, Tobacco. • Trees: Cedarwood, Juniper, Almond. • Herbs: Bay Leaf, Bergamot, Mint, Lavender, Thyme.	**Planets** • Mercury

Death

GONE YOU ARE

Your body is cold,

Your hand I hold.

You lie there still,

You weren't even ill.

I am in shock,

I can hear every tick of the clock.

Gone you are, never to return,

To live without you:
Is something I must now learn.

Safe Journey Ritual & Charm

This is a long ritual and Spell. But it's worth the time as the effects are long lasting. For this ritual you will need:

- A bell.
- X3 White Candles.
- X1 yellow Candle.
- X1 Bronzite crystal.
- X1 Danburite crystal.
- X1 Amethyst point.
- X2 Blue Angelite crystals.
- X1 Citrine point.
- X3 Smokey Quartz Points.
- X1 Clear Quartz crystal.
- Patchouli essential oil.
- Lemongrass essential oil.
- Oil burner.
- Herbs - Lavender, Chamomile and Cinnamon.
- Photo of the deceased.
- A piece of card.
- Glue.
- A Black Charm Bag.
- Compass (for elemental directions).

1. Cleanse and charge each of the crystals, ideally on a Full Moon.

2. Stick the photo of the deceased on a piece of card and write on the card:

[name of deceased] be Protected.
[name of deceased] be Healed.
[name of deceased] Communicate.
[name of deceased] be Happy and Joyful.

This is now your Words of Power Card, put to one side for use later on.

3. Cleanse space - hoovering, dusting, tidying, etc.

4. Cleanse self - ritual bath, visualising your aura and body being fully cleansed.

5. Put an elemental representation in each corner of the room:
- North, Earth: Quartz Crystal

- East, Air: Bell

- South, Fire: x1 white candle, lit

- West, Water: oil burner with Patchouli oil burning

- Use compass for elemental directions

6. Gather together items for charm bag:
- Crystals: X1 Bronzite crystal, X1 Danburite crystal, X1 Amethyst point, X2 Blue Angelite crystals, X1 Citrine point, X3 Smokey Quartz Points.

- Herbs: Those to dispel negativity and for protection. Lavender, Chamomile & Cinnamon.

- Candle: x1 yellow

- Oils: Lemongrass and Patchouli

- Photo of the deceased.

- Chant cart with Words of Power

- Charm Bag

7. Casting the Circle, calling of the quarters. Go to the North. Hold the Quartz crystal in the air and say:

Hail to the watchtowers of the North, Powers of Mother Earth. Hail and Welcome.

Visualise a green pillar of energy come from the depths of the earth.

Go to the East. Ring the bell once and say:

Hail to the watchtowers of the East, Powers of Air and Intellect, Hail and Welcome.

Visualise a yellow pillar of energy come from all around the air around you.

Go to the South. Light the candle and say:

Hail to the watchtowers of the South, Powers of Fire and Passion, Hail and Welcome.

Visualise a red pillar of energy come from the flame of the candle.

Go to the West. See the oil burner and say:

Hail to the watchtowers of the West, Powers of Water and Emotion, Hail and Welcome.

Visualise a blue pillar of energy come from the oil burner.

Then say:

As above, so below.

Join the pillars of energy together to create a circle, then turn it into a bubble of protection by joining the top and bottom of the circle.

8. Welcome the Goddess and God. Light one white candle and say:

Hail and Welcome to the Goddess in all her forms. I ask that you provide protection and aid me in this magical working.

Light the other white candle and say:
Hail and welcome to the God in all his forms. I ask that you provide protection and aid me in this magical working.

9. Line the pouch with a small amount of Lemongrass oil and say:

With this scent of smell, I cleanse and protect this pouch and all of its contents.

10. Hold herbs in hand and breathe life and energy into them. State intention by saying:

Banish negativity and protect [name of deceased]'s mind, body and spirit.

Put in charm bag and breathe more life into the herbs by taking two deep breaths and exhaling into the bag.

11. Take the Bronzite for Protection. Go into the crystal. Visualise [name of deceased]'s soul being protected by a brown energy. See the stones energy changing to undertake this eternal task. Say the statement of intent:

Bronzite, protect [name of deceased]'s soul Forever.
The protection end Never.
Let him/her be Safe.
As within, let it be without.

Anoint with Patchouli Oil, place in the charm bag.

12. Take the Amethyst for Healing. Go into the crystal. Visualise [name of deceased]'s soul being healed. See any grey or damaged parts being penetrated by a purple light until it is a pure white colour. Say the statement of intent:

Ancient Amethyst crystal heal [name of deceased]'s soul.

Let all illness and disease be eradicated.
As it is within, let it be without.

Anoint with Patchouli Oil, place in the charm bag.

13. Take one of the Blue Angelite for Telepathic
Communication. Go into the stone. Visualise [name of
deceased] being able to communicate with all beings.
Humans, guardian spirits, etc. Visualise him/her on all
planes of existence communicating well. Visualising
him/her talking as he/she did. Say the statement of
intent:

Angelite ensure that [name of deceased] can communicate
with all on all levels of existence.
Let him/her talk and express himself/herself well.
As within, let it be without.

Anoint with Patchouli Oil.

Take the other blue Angelite stone. Go into the stone.
Visualise it linked to the other and [name of deceased]
able to use it as a link to communicate. See the stones
linked, eternally. Say the statement of intent:

Angelite stone, you are forever connected to this one.

Take the first Angelite stone in your hand and continue:

Your purpose is to enable [name of deceased] to
communicate with the physical world.

As within, let it be without.

Anoint with Patchouli Oil. Hold the crystals together before placing the first crystal in the charm bag.

14. Take the Citrine point for Happiness & Joy. Go into the stone. Visualise [name of deceased] happy. See them laughing, joking, smiling. Feel your happiness that he/she is happy and send this into the stone. See the Citrine glow brightly with yellow, happy energy. Say the statement of intent:

Your purpose is to fill [name of decreased]'s soul with Happiness and Joy.
Let him laugh, smile and cry with joy like he/she once did.
As within, let it be without.

Anoint with Patchouli Oil, place in the charm bag.

15. Take the Danburite for Safe Journey. Go into the stone. Visualise [name of deceased]'s soul journeying where ever it wishes safely. See no barriers - not even space or time. Say the statement of intent:

Danburite your purpose is to allow [name of deceased]'s soul to travel safely.
Let no barriers, not even space, time and distance get in his/her way,
Aid [name of deceased]'s transition to the afterlife, now do as I say.

As within, let it be without.

Anoint with Patchouli Oil, place in the charm bag.

16. Take each Smokey Quartz crystal as chargers and amplifiers. Go into each stone. Visualise each Smokey Quartz collecting energy from the infinite energy of the Earth and see it transferring this energy to all the crystals in the charm bag. Then visualise each Smokey Quartz enhancing the transmission of the energy by the crystals. See the energy go into the deep depths of the universe. Say the statement of intent:

Smokey Quartz Crystals you are energisers. Collect energy from mother Earth from which you came and transmit it to the other crystals and stones around you. Amplify their energies to enable them to complete their tasks. Their tasks are eternal as is yours.

As within, let it be without.

Anoint the crystals with Patchouli Oil, place in the charm bag.

17. Anoint the yellow candle with lemongrass to light [name of deceased]'s way. Say:

This will light your way.
From the dark and cold afterlife.
Rest in peace your body may.
But your soul be alive as ever.

Protected. Healed. Able to Communicate. Happy and Joyful.
Your journey be a safe one.

Drop Wax from the candle into the charm bag.

18. Spiral of Power. Walk in a clockwise direction around the circle chanting:

[name of deceased] be Protected.
[name of deceased] be Healed.
[name of deceased] Communicate.
[name of deceased] be Happy and Joyful.

Visualise all the energy you create with walking and chanting flow in a spiral quicker and quicker. Then with a hand movement push the spiral of power into the charm bag. Know that the energy has its purpose and understands what it must do.

19. Place your Words of Power card in the charm bag and seal.

20. Close the circle by saying hail, farewell and thanks to the Goddess, God and elemental quarters. To finish say something like:

The circle is now open. The rite complete. As I will it, so mote it be. As I will it, so MUST it be.

21. The best place to place the charm bag is ideally on

the body of the deceased. Think about putting it in a pocket. Alternatively, it can be buried close by to the grave.

Death Correspondences

Colours	Crystals
• Black • Dark Purple • Dark Blue	• Amethyst • Danburite • Kunzite • Kyanite • Opal
Days of the Week	**Elements**
• Sunday • Wednesday • Saturday	• Earth • Fire
Essential Oils	**Phase(s) of The Moon**
• Cypress • Cardamom • Frankincense • Ginger • Myrrh • Sandalwood	• Dark Moon
Herbs, Trees & Plants	**Planets**
• Plants: Lilly & Poppy. • Trees: Yew Tree, Italian Cypress, Elder, Willow. • Herbs: Laurel & Mandrake.	• Pluto

Employment

TOMORROW'S CHANCE

Is there a place for me out there?

Is there a task for me to do?

Am I looking in the wrong place?

Am I sure of what to do?

Will tomorrow bring new challenges?

Will tomorrow bring a chance?

I only ask for guidance.

Please help me understand.

General Gain Employment Spell

Need a job to pay the bills? Use this general gain employment Spell. For this spell you will need:

- X1 Yellow candle.
- X1 Pebble.
- X1 Small pot paint or nail varnish.
- X1 Brush.

1. Light the yellow candle and say:

Shining light look kindly upon me.

2. Hold the pebble in your hands and looking at the candle flame imagine yourself happy, working in a job you would like to do and having money. After a few moments of concentration gently blow onto the stone and imagine all your positive thoughts going into the stone and say:

Stone of the earth, I charge you.

3. Paint this symbol onto the stone and leave it next to the candle to dry:

4. When the stone is dry you carry it with you.

5. When you have achieved your goal of employment, discard the stone by throwing it into the nearest fresh water supply.

A New Moon Spell for a Specific New Job

This Spell works to land you your ideal job. It should be used with a specific job in mind. For this spell you will need:

- A yellow candle.
- An oil to anoint the candle.
- Something to scratch/mark the candle. We used scissors.
- To have a specific job in mind.

1. Before a new moon, scratch/mark the yellow candle with the initials of the job title for the job you want.

2. Charge the candle with energy of your own.

See the golden energy moved down from your head, into your heart and then down your arm and into the candle in your hand. Imagine being offered the job and feel the happiness and excitement when it happens. Send the image of you being offered the job from your head into the candle. Feel the happiness and excitement in your heart and send that down and into the candle. Repeat this visualisation least 12 times. This should take you several minutes.

3. Anoint the candle with oil to seal in the energy.

4. On the first day of the new moon, say the following as you light the candle and repeat 9 times:

Make the (job title) job mine,
Let me be great at the job and my talents shine.
Let me interview well, myself I sell,
Let me be the best there is!
Let the money come in,
And may I enjoy it with a grin.
As the Moon does grow,
Let the magic in this spell flow,
Release it into the cosmos slow and steady,
So that everything falls in to place and is ready.
As I will it, so it is.

5. Burn the candle over several days. Each time you relight the candle, repeat the words above.

To Attract New Employment Opportunities Bath Oil

Want to attract some new employment opportunities into your life? This bath oil and corresponding Spell are the ultimate attraction formula to bring new employment opportunities. For this spell you will need:

- Patchouli essential oil.
- Vetiver essential oil.
- Cypress essential oil.
- Juniper essential oil.
- Base oil.

1. Make up the oil using the following formula:

- 12 drops of Patchouli essential oil.
- 6 drops of Vetiver essential oil.
- 12 drops of Cypress essential oil.
- 6 drops of Juniper essential oil.
- 10mls of Base oil.

2. Put 2-5 drops in the bath under the hot tap and say:

Gaia, mother of all,
Here my call!
Bring new opportunities to me,
From this day forth, so mote it be.

A Charm To Gain A Promotion

Want or need a promotion at work? This charm will bring one along quickly. For this spell you will need:

- A green charm bag.
- Sunflower seeds.
- Sage (herb).
- Chamomile flowers (dried).
- Bloodstone crystal.
- Black Obsidian crystal.
- Aventurine (green) crystal.
- A piece of yellow felt.
- A marker pen.
- Bergamot essential oil.
- Sandalwood essential oil.
- Base oil.
- An empty essential oils bottle, ideally one with a pipette.

1. Make up the charm bag:

- X3 Sunflower seeds
- A pinch of Sage (herb).
- X2 teaspoons of Chamomile flowers (dried).
- X1 Bloodstone crystal.
- X1 Black obsidian crystal.
- X1 Aventurine (green) crystal.

2. Cut the yellow felt into the shape of a coin (round) and

draw the symbol for Mercury on it using the marker pen. The symbol for Mercury looks like this:

3. Put the felt coin into the charm bag.

4. Next make up the oil and pour it into the empty essential oil bottle:

- X5 drops of Bergamot essential oil.
- X5 drops of Sandalwood essential oil.
- 5mls of Base oil.

5. Each day 'feed' your charm bag a drop of the oil and say:

Mercury bring to me my deserved promotion.
Let this cause no commotion.
As I will it, so mote it be.

6. Once you have gained your promotion bury the charm bag in the earth and give thanks.

Successful Interview Oil

This oil should be worn on the day of your interview as a perfume or aftershave. The formula is as follows:

- X3 drops of Ylang Ylang.
- X2 drops of Lavender.
- X4 drops of Rosewood.
- 5mls of Base Oil.

Employment Correspondences

Colours	Crystals
• Orange • Gold • Yellow • Purple	• Loadstone • Black Obsidian • Bloodstone
Days of the Week	**Elements**
• Sunday • Tuesday • Thursday	• Earth • Air
Essential Oils	**Phase(s) of The Moon**
• Jasmine • Bergamot • Ylang Ylang	• New Moon • Full Moon
Herbs, Trees & Plants	**Planets**
• Plants: Ivy. • Trees: Birch, Pine, Apple. • Herbs: Cloves, Bay, Bayberry, Pine.	• Mars • Jupiter

Finance & Money

I WANT IT ALL

I want it all I want it now.

That's all I seem to hear.

I need it I should have it.

Why are these words so clear.

Accept there is a time and place.

For everything to come,

But if your chasing rainbows.

Then your work is never done.

A Note on Money Magic

Money magic is an area of magic that can be fraught with difficulty and complications if you don't follow the following principles:

1. Only ask for the amount you need. Asking for more than you need, say a large amount of money, often doesn't work. When it does, in our experience, you'll get exactly what you asked for, but it may come as inheritance after the death of a loved relative.

Asking to win a large amount on the lottery never works. The odds are too great. If this is your aim you are likely to need a large amount of luck magic as well as money magic. The amount of energy to manifest something with millions to one odds are likely to make you severely ill and for this reason we would not recommend that you try it.

2. Don't use harm none, but do use without serious injury or death. Many practitioners use harm none in all of their magic and this often derails their own magic. Antony once did a spell for money and found a twenty-pound note on the ground the next day. If Antony had put harm none, this wouldn't have happened. As someone had to lose the twenty pound in order for Antony to find it - to put it bluntly someone had to be harmed by the loss of twenty pound in order for Antony to find it.

That written we would never want anyone to be seriously injured or die due to our magic. So rather than using harm none, use without serious injury or death in Spells.

3. Do be specific with the reason you need the money. Asking for money for money's sake is usually ineffective magic. This is because often there's no strong intention, strong will or strong emotion to power the Spell. So in all your money magic, do be specific with the reason for needing the money.

4. Don't be afraid to use money magic for luxuries, just be sure to be realistic. Money is supposed to buy more than the necessities of life. It is supposed to be used for luxuries as well. So, it's fine to do Spells that ask for the money for luxuries. Just be sure to ask for a bit extra on top, so that you can make a small donation to charity to give something back.

5. Don't rely on money magic to get you out of an urgent debt. Long term money magic to reduce or get you out of debt is fine. But don't rely on money magic to get you out of a short-term urgent debt. Instead follow the rule: if you can't afford to pay it back, especially as a short-term loan, then don't borrow it.

It's fine to do an Emergency! Quick Cash money Spell, in fact we've included one in this section. Try that instead.

Malachite For Money
Carry a piece of Malachite in your purse or wallet to attract money. Be sure to cleanse it before use and charge it with your intention. This Spell will last about a month before the Malachite needs recharging.

A New Moon Spell for Money
For this spell you will need:

- A green candle.
- Patchouli essential oil.
- Gold, Silver and Green Glitter.
- Green Paper.
- A Green Pen.

1. Start the Spell on a new moon.

2. Take the green paper. Write on the amount of money you require and what you need the money for. This is your Money Talisman.

3. Anoint the candle by rubbing Patchouli essential oil into the candle, starting from the middle and working to the ends. Then sprinkle on glitter saying:

All that glistens is silver and gold,
bring to me [state amount of money] to hold.

4. Place the candle and the money talisman 10-12 inches apart on a table or shelf where it will be safe and can be left for the next few days. Light the candle and say:

Money drawing - money come - money needed - and it seriously injury or kill none.

5. Sit for a while watching the candle flame. Imagine yourself having the money and using it in the necessary way.

6. Finally move the candle a little closer to the money

talisman and say:

The charm is set - bring money to me,
By sun and moon,
So mote it be.

7. Repeat steps 5 & 6 over the next few nights until the candle is eventually on top of the money talisman. Then let the candle burn down fully.

8. Carry the talisman with you in your purse/wallet until you receive the money you need. Then burn the talisman and give thanks.

Emergency! Quick Cash Spell
Need cash in a hurry? Then this is the Spell for you. For this spell you will need:

- £1 or $1 in change.
- X1 box - nicely decorated.
- X1 green ribbon.

1. Start the Spell by summoning forth Baccus:

Baccus bringer of good times I ask that you hear me.
Money I need, but only [amount of money needed], I ask thee.
This [amount of money] I need fast,
and my gratitude will ever last.

2. Put the money into the box saying:

As I put this money in this container let it grow,
Make money more than the amount low.

Now multiple this money by [number for the amount
required, (i.e. fifteen)],
and make it come before tomorrow night has been.

Now I give my energies to this Spell,
So that it will work well.

3. Tie the ribbon around the box saying:

As I tie the ribbon the spell be bound,
The Spell is cast, and takes effect.

4. Then sing to the box:

Money Money Money, Mon-ey,
(x9 times)

5. Now say:

The Spell is done,
make it work during the light of the sun.

So mote it be.

Financial Security Charm

This Spell will bring financial security into your life. For this spell you will need:

- Orchid Roots.
- X3 Aventurine crystals.
- Clove Herb.
- Basil Herb.
- Cinnamon Herb.
- X1 small sunflower head.
- X1 Sunflower seed.
- Bergamot essential oil.
- Patchouli essential oil.
- A £1 Coin or other currency.
- A Gold or Silver charm bag.

1. Place the following into the charm bag:

- X1 teaspoon of Orchid Roots
- X3 Aventurine crystals
- 1/2 a teaspoon of Clove
- X1 Teaspoon of Basil
- X1 Teaspoon of Cinnamon
- X1 small Sunflower head
- X1 Sunflower seed
- X3 drops of Bergamot essential oil.
- X3 drops of Patchouli oil.
- £1 coin or other currency.

2. Close the bag and say three times:
Bring me financial stability,
Bring me money security.
Empower this charm and let there be,
Money for the future me.

Reduce Debt Spell

This Spell is a long-term spell that will reduce the amount of debt you have. For this spell you will need:

- A green candle.
- A knife.
- X1 Citrine crystal.
- Basil (herb).
- Cinnamon essential oil.
- Cypress essential oil.
- Patchouli essential oil.
- Bergamot essential oil.
- Base oil.

1. Make up the oil:

- X1 pinch of Basil Herb
- X3 drops of Cinnamon.
- X3 drops of Cypress.
- X3 drops of Patchouli.
- X3 drops of Bergamot.
- 5mls of base oil.

2. Using the knife carve the symbol of your currency (e.g., £ or $) and an arrow pointing down.

3. Anoint your candle with the oil.

4. Anoint bank cards, any credit cards and your wallet with the oil.

5. Light the candle and chant six times:

Powers of Fire and Air hear me,
Reduce my debt I ask of thee.
Let it dwindle and disappear,
Until I owe nothing to anyone.
So shall it be.

6. Anoint the Citrine crystal with the left over oil and put it in the wealth corner of your home.

7. **Never** wash the oil off your hands. Instead allow to dry.

Business Success Spell
Run your own business? This Spell will help it prosper. For this spell you will need:

- Basil (herb).
- Cinnamon essential oil.
- Cypress essential oil.
- Patchouli essential oil.
- Bergamot essential oil.
- Base oil.
- X1 Gold candle.

- An Aventurine crystal.
- A Loadstone crystal.
- A green charm bag.

1. Make up the oil:

- X1 pinch of Basil Herb.
- X3 drops of Cinnamon essential oil.
- X3 drops of Cypress essential oil.
- X3 drops of Patchouli essential oil.
- X3 drops of Bergamot essential oil.
- 5mls of base oil.

2. Charge the candle and anoint it with the oil.

3. Charge the Aventurine and Loadstone crystals with your intention, anoint with the oil and place in the green charm bag.

4. Anoint the business bank card, credit card and/or a business card with the oil.

5. Light the candle. Chant the following six times over the candle, charm bag, cards and what remains of the oil:

Money grow, money flow,
Business prosper now.
Money come without delay,
Start my/our earning today.
So shall it be.

6. Put the charm bag in the place of business. If it is an

online business keep it near your computer.

7. If possible, use the left over oil to anoint the business premises.

Money Problems Solved For A Whole Year
A Witch Bottle for money is a brilliant way to solve money problems for a whole year. And even beyond. For this spell you will need:

- X1 small bottle.
- Basil (herb).
- Cinnamon essential oil.
- Cypress essential oil.
- Patchouli essential oil.
- Bergamot essential oil.
- Base oil.
- X3 small green crystals.
- X1 small Rose Quartz crystal.
- X1 small Carnelian crystal.
- X1 Green piece of paper.
- A pen.
- Green glitter.
- X3 small mirrors.
- Some of your hair or finger/toe nail clippings.
- X1 Brown Candle.
- X1 Orange Candle.
- X1 Yellow Candle.
- Rose Water (if required).

1. Make up the oil:

- X1 pinch of Basil Herb
- X3 drops of Cinnamon essential oil.
- X3 drops of Cypress essential oil.
- X3 drops of Patchouli essential oil.
- X3 drops of Bergamot essential oil.
- 5mls of base oil.

2. Put the oil, the x3 small green crystals, the rose quartz, the carnelian, some green glitter, the tiny mirrors, some of your hair and/or nail clippings in the bottle.

3. On the green paper use the pen to draw the rune for growth, it looks like this:

4. The cut the paper to size so it fits in the bottle.

5. Drip x6 drops of wax from the brown, orange and yellow candles into the bottle.

6. Top up with Rose Water if required.

7. Seal the bottle using wax from the three candles. Place

the bottle in the wealth corner of your home.

Finance & Money Correspondences

Colours	Crystals
• Green • Gold • Brown • Orange	• Citrine • Malachite • Aventurine • Moss Agate (Green) • Jade (Green) • Loadstone
Days of the Week	**Elements**
• Thursday • Sunday • Saturday	• Earth • Water • Fire
Essential Oils	**Phase(s) of The Moon**
• Bergamot • Cypress • Ginger • Jasmine • Orange • Rosemary • Patchouli	• New Moon • Full Moon
Herbs, Trees & Plants	**Planets**
• Plants: Anise, Basil, Narcissus. • Trees: Cypress, Honeysuckle. Primrose, Fern. Any evergreen. • Herbs: Sage, Basil, Cinnamon.	• Jupiter • Mercury

Fertility

FERTILITY

As the new moon starts to form, In the blackness of the night.

Let the seeds of life empower, You with the gift of life.

A simple act of love can set the spell in motion,

And as the moon begins to grow so too the new devotion.

Embrace the life within you and let the magic flow,

And as the moon waxes full give thanks as you both grow.

Like the new growth in the Springtime prepare for warmer days.

Cherish every moment of the new life you will treasure.

And when the day of birth arrives give thanks for all that's been.

And face a future filled with love, hope and dreams.

The Apple Seed Conception Spell
For this spell you will need:

- An apple.
- A Moonstone crystal.
- A small plant pot with compost.

1. On the night of A New Moon take an apple and cut across the middle to reveal the pips in the centre forming a pentagram. Place a Moonstone on the center. Say three times:

Mother Nature hear my plea,
Fill me with Fertility.
Charge this stone and these seeds.
Help them bring me what I need.

2. Place the Moonstone in the pot of compost in the center remove the seeds from the apple and plant them around the Moonstone. As you plant each seed say:

Into the womb goes the seed
Mother earth help me conceive.

3. Place the pot on a warm windowsill and water the seeds.

4. When the moon is full take the Moonstone and keep it with you.

5. When you do conceive plant the seeds outside and give thanks.

Conception Poppet (for Women)
For this spell you will need:

- A pack of air drying clay.
- x1 green candle.

1. Make a figure to represent yourself adding some of your own hair or fingernails, or whatever represents you.

2.Make an indentation in the belly of the poppet.

3. Light the green candle, line the indentation with wax from the candle and say:

Grant me power to conceive,
Mother nature hear my plea,
Make me fertile like the earth,
Keep us safe throughout the birth.

4. Make a small poppet to represent a child, lay it on the green wax and say:

From the earth all things grow,
To my womb let new life flow.
Mother nature hear my plea,
Grant me power to conceive.

5. Keep both poppets safe until you conceive. Then bury them in the earth and give thanks.

Conception Spell (for Male)

For this spell you will need:

- Some air drying clay.
- A small white candle.

1. Make a phallus that will stand erect and place the small white candle in the end.

2. When the clay has dried hard, wait for the next New Moon. Then light the candle and say:

All the powers of Earth and Sky,
Give my seed the wings to fly.
Give my seed the strength to swim,
To penetrate the eggs within.
Make me fertile, make me potent,
Charge me from this very moment.
Lord and Lady grant my plea,
A father will you make of me.

3. Leave the candle to burn down and if possible make love while the candle burns.

4. Keep the phallus by your bed (or under it) until conception. Then bury in the earth and give thanks.

Fertility Correspondences

Colours	Crystals
• Green • Pink • Apple	• Unakite • Moonstone • Carnelian • Amber • Topaz • Jadeite
Days of the Week	**Elements**
• Friday • Sunday • Monday	• Water • Earth
Essential Oils	**Phase(s) of The Moon**
• Star Anise • Lavender • Rosemary • Basil	• New Moon
Herbs, Trees & Plants	**Planets**
• Plants: Mistletoe, Poppy, Grape, Rose. • Trees: Chestnut, Catkins & Bradford Pear, Coconut, Apple Tree, Pine. • Herbs: Basil.	• Moon • Venus

Friendship

ANOTHER SPECIAL YEAR.

There's a feeling I get when I look to the west,

that reminds me of all that we've shared.

It's not just the song, though it's one of the best,

it's the memories and stories we've heard.

Pathways we travelled, adventures we had,

and sacred paths trodden in awe.

It's not just the knowing you makes me so glad,

It's the knowledge there will be much more.

We've painted great murals, embroidered vast tales,

and stitched holes in the fabric of time.

Enjoyed our successes and most of our fails,

for we are like partners in crime.

We've slept in the wilderness, swam in the seas,

rubbed shoulders with giants and witch Queens.

Danced in the circles like a swift summer breeze,

and slept through the strangest of dreams.

We've given love freely and received in return,

enough love to keep on just giving.

We've studied the scriptures and took what we learned,

and molded our own way of living.

Now another year passes and we mark once again,

how lucky we are and how blessed.

And that feeling is there in the wind and the rain.

When I stop and I look to the west.

A Friendship Attraction Oil

This oil can be worn, used in a bath or burned in an oil burner. This attraction oil is great for attracting new friends. For this attraction oil you will need:

- Sandalwood essential oil.
- Ylang Ylang essential oil.
- Jasmine essential oil.
- Base oil.

1. Make up the oil:

- X6 drops of Sandalwood essential oil.
- X3 drops of Ylang Ylang essential oil.
- X5 drops of Jasmine essential oil.
- 5mls Base oil.

2. Wear the oil, use in a bath or in an oil burner.

Repairing a Friendship Ritual

For this ritual you will need:

- Picture of you and your friend together (happier times).
- A yellow candle.
- Two white candles.
- Friendship oil (see friendship attraction oil above).
- Two Loadstone crystals.

- A red ribbon.
- An orange piece of material.

1. Cast a circle in the usual way.

2. Welcome the God and Goddess lighting a white candle for each deity saying:

Gracious Goddess come hear my plea,
Bring my best friend back to me.
Glorious God hear my plea,
Repair the friendship I ask of thee.

3. Charge the yellow candle. Visualise the two of you becoming close again. Imagine how this will make you feel and embrace the energy and let it flow into the candle.

4. Anoint the candle with the friendship oil from the centre outward to the ends.

5. Light the yellow candle saying:

Flame that flickers and glows,
Repair our friendship woes.
Bring happiness back for you and me,
Rekindle our love for all to see.

6. Allow the candle to burn down fully whilst meditating on the picture and visualising your desired results.

7. When the candle is almost done. Take the picture and the two Loadstone crystals. Wrap them in the orange fabric and say:

I bring you close my dear friend,
From now until our times end.

Come together and never part,
For you are here within my heart.

8. Bind the parcel with the red ribbon and close the circle. Keep the parcel safe or give it to your friend as a gift of love.

9. Give thanks and close the circle.

Get New Friends Fast Spell
For this spell you will need:

- X1 piece of felt in the following colours: yellow, orange, red, pink, bright blue, bright green.
- A Marker Pen.
- A yellow ribbon.
- Juniper essential oil.
- Ylang Ylang essential oil.
- Grapefruit essential oil.

1. Cut each piece of felt down to a small size and using the marker pen write an attribute of the friend(s) you

wish to attract (e.g. they must love music, enjoy nature, be kind, be compassionate, etc.).

2. Make up the oil by using:

- X3 drops of Juniper essential oil.
- X3 drops of Ylang Ylang essential oil.
- X3 drops of Grapefruit essential oil.

3. Add a few drops of the oil mix to each piece of felt.

4.Next thread the felt pieces through the yellow ribbon, tying a knot at each end.

5. Hang this in the friendship corner of your home. The friendship corner of your home is in the North West direction.

To Create Lasting Friendships
For this spell you will need:

- 18 inches of white wool
- 18 inches of wool in your favourite colour to represent you.
- 18 inches of wool in your friend's favourite colour to represent them.
- Scissors.

1. Knot the three pieces together at one end.

2. Braid until you have enough to go round your friend's wrist. Then tie a knot in the end and using the scissors cut off any excess.

3. Tie around your friend's wrist to symbolise your friendship.

4. Repeat the above to make yourself a bracelet and have your friend tie it round your wrist.

5. Then over the bracelets say:

From the same substance we are made. Separate but we are the same.

Eternal circle bind our hearts, so that we might never part.

Friendship Correspondences

Colours	Crystals
• Yellow • Orange • Red • Pink • Bright Blue • Bright Green	• Snowflake Obsidian • Garnet • Lapis Lazuli • Smithsonite
Days of the Week	**Elements**
• Sunday • Tuesday • Wednesday	• Air • Water
Essential Oils	**Phase(s) of The Moon**
• Patchouli • Juniper • Cedarwood • Benzoin • Grapefruit • Ylang Ylang	• Any • Even better if you can work in sunlight.
Herbs, Trees & Plants	**Planets**
• Plants: Lavender. • Trees: Pine. • Herbs: Mugwort.	• Jupiter • Sun • Mars • Mercury

Happiness & Joy

KNOWING THAT I AM LOVED

To sit by open water will always make me smile,

The peacefulness and harmony soothes me for a while.

To watch the wild stags rutting sets fire in my soul,

The power and the majesty makes my spirit whole.

To hear the birds each morning sing a chorus clear,

The sweet sounds of birdsong always brings me cheer.

To feel the grass beneath my feet to touch the morning dew,

To help me feel the joy of life this is what I do.

To know that every night I sleep knowing I am loved,

Brings happiness to every day as every day it should.

A Happiness Spell
Need some happiness in your life? Then cast this Spell.
For this spell you will need:

- A citrine crystal point.

1. Cleanse and charge a citrine crystal point.

2. Case a circle and raise power chanting:

Power of love, power of light,
Positive energy come on this night.

3. Take a moment to feel that the energy has built up,
feel the love and positivity in the energy, feel how happy
it makes you.

4. Take the citrine point (so the point is point towards
your heart), go clockwise visualising the energy being
drawn into your heart chakra.

5. See the energy flow from your heart to the citrine
point as you say these words:

Citrine bright as a summers sun,
Bring me happiness and bring me fun.
True happiness is all I ask on this night,
Bring what I've asked into my sight.
Power of Citrine this is your task,
Show me the path to happiness is all that I ask.
Now bring happiness to me! So I will it, so it is.

A Happiness & Money Spell
This Spell is highly effective and we have nicknamed it the Master Bringer of All Spell. For this Spell you will need:

- A yellow candle.
- A green candle.
- A paper and pen.
- Sandalwood essential oil.
- A fire proof dish.

1. Charge the yellow candle for happiness and the green candle for money. Anoint each candle after charging with sandalwood oil.

2. Write out the following spell on a piece of paper:

By the Dragon's light,
On this [month] night,
Bring happiness and money into sight.

Let [name]'s life be filled with joy,
Every task he/she does enjoy.
With happiness in his/her heart,
Any sadness and pain does now depart.

Let [name] claim monies owed,
Until monies he/she has bestowed.
He/she will not worry about money,
For it shall flow freely like honey.

By the Dragon's light,

On this [month] night.

[Name] you are happy.
[Name] you have money.
By the Dragon's might.
So mote it be.

3. When you are ready light both candles, say the spell aloud and then burn the piece of paper with the words written on to release the spell into the cosmos.

If doing this spell for yourself say *for myself* where the name is.

If you are doing the spell for someone else make sure to imagine them happy and with money.

4. Allow the candles to burn down, releasing the intentioned energy out into the universe.

A Positive Spell
For this Spell, all you need is a candle, ideally white.

Sit somewhere comfortable, where you can spend some quiet time visualising without interruption. Take the candle in-between your hands and close your eyes.

Clear your mind of all thoughts, forget about the pressures and stresses of the day. Visualise a treasure chest in your mind and see all of your thoughts as coloured light. See the chest open and absorb all of the coloured light, until all that is left is your clear mind.

Now, think of what would make your life and those

around you more positive, more fulfilled and happier. It maybe job security or more money, more time with loved ones, improved health, time to be creative, whatever it is, spend at least 10 minutes visualising this in as much detail as you can.

See it actually happening in your mind and imagine how people you know respond when you tell them the news. Then visualise all these thoughts as yellow energy and visualise the energy move from your brain down to your heart.

Now visualise how you will feel when what you have visualised happens. Feel green positive, warm, bright energy of your emotions join your yellow thought energy.

Now see this mass of positive energy flow down your arms, in to your hands and then penetrate and fill the candle. The candle should almost seem to glow with a warm, positive energy.

Each night light the candle for roughly an hour, saying as you light the candle:

Release the energy within, like attract like.
Positive energy attract positive things in to my life.

A Gift of Happiness for Others

Buy your friend or family member a nice gift. An ideal gift for this Spell is a luxury candle that corresponds with happiness. That way, when they light the candle, they'll be performing candle magic without even realising it. For this spell you will need:

- A gift for the person you are casting the spell on, ideally a candle.

1. Charge the gift with these words of power said three times:

Happiness come, happiness flow.
Happiness come, happiness grow.

Make [name] as happy as can be,
[Name]'s happiness all shall see.

Let [name] be healthy.
Let [name] be wealthy.
Let [name] be in love.
Let [name] be protected by Angels above.
As I will it, so it shall be. As I will it deep in my heart, so it is.

2. Give the gift to your friend or family member and watch for results.

A Joyous Charm
We all need a little joy in our lives from time to time. This powerful attraction charm will attract more joy into your life. For this spell you will need:

- A yellow charm bag.
- A Citrine, Rose Quartz and Topaz crystals.
- Cinnamon essential oil.
- Cedarwood essential oil.
- Orange essential oil.
- Cypress essential oil.
- Rose petals (dried).
- Star Anise (dried).
- A sunflower seed.

1. Make up the charm bag with the following ingredients:

- A Citrine crystal.
- A Rose Quartz crystal.
- A Topaz crystal.
- X1 drop of Cinnamon essential oil.
- X1 drop of Cedarwood essential oil.
- X2 drops of Orange essential oil.
- X3 Star Anise (dried).
- X6 Rose petals (dried).

2. Carry the charm bag with you to attract joy.

Respect Yourself Bath

Feeling a need for respect? Make up this bath oil and bathe in it regularly. Make up the following oil and pour six drops of it under the hot tap when running a bath:

- X8 drops of Juniper essential oil.
- X6 drops of Cedar essential oil.
- X3 drops of Cinnamon essential oil.
- 10mls of Base oil.

1. Repeat as necessary.

Feel Good Oil

Wear this oil to feel good about yourself and your life:

- X1 drop of Spearmint essential oil.
- X9 drops of Orange essential oil.
- X9 drops of Frankincense essential oil.
- X3 drops of Star Anise essential oil.
- 10mls of Base oil.

Happiness & Joy Correspondences

Colours	Crystals
• Yellow • Gold • Pink • White • Dark Blue	• Citrine • Jasper • Topaz • Rose Quartz • Rhodonite • Dioptase
Days of the Week	**Elements**
• Sunday • Wednesday	• Water • Fire
Essential Oils	**Phase(s) of The Moon**
• Cinnamon • Cedarwood • Frankincense • Orange • Spearmint • Thyme	• New Moon • Full Moon
Herbs, Trees & Plants	**Planets**
• Plants: Sunflower, Anise. • Trees: Cypress, Bay, Olive. • Herbs: Bay Leaf, Cinnamon and Ginger.	• Jupiter • Sun

Health

A FIELD OF DREAMS FOR PEACE

Look high and see the mother moon.

Embraced by father sky.

Watching over me and you,

As we let our hopes take flight,

A vision of a future bright.

A longing for release.

Where everyone is equal.

A field of dreams for peace.

Come take my hand and walk with me,

Along a path that's wide.

Wide enough for everyone,

Each faith stood side by side.

The time has come to make a stand.

The time for pain has ceased.

Here everyone is equal.

A field of dreams for peace.

Break all the chains that bind you,

For we all can be free.

Free to share the wonders,

Of the grass beneath our feet.

Embark with me upon a voyage,

On seas and oceans deep.

Where everyone is equal.

A field of dreams for peace.

A vast unbroken circle,

A spiral ever turning.

A place of quiet reflection,

A home of spiritual learning.

A place of love and harmony,

A sanctuary free from grief.

Where everyone is equal.

A field of dreams for peace.

A Note on Health Craft

Please note that the Spells in this section are intended to be used **alongside** following advice from your General Practitioner, Specialist Consultants and other Health Professionals. These Spells should **never** be used instead of seeking medical advice and treatment, under any circumstances.

A Good Health Crystal Charm

This charm will maintain or bring good health to you. You will need:

- 1 Aventurine Crystal.
- 1 Tiger's Eye Crystal.

1. Cleanse and charge the crystals.

2. Chant:

Heal me, Heal me, Heal me

3. As you chant visualise the part of your body that needs healing and overall good health.

This spell will last one month, before the crystals will require recharging. This can be used for mental or emotional pain as well as physical pain. Just swap the crystals for more appropriate ones. This spell can also be used on others to promote recovery from poor health and to boost overall health.

Anxiety & Depression Bath and Spell

Anxiety and depression are severe mental illnesses. We wanted to create something that is easy, yet effective at alleviating symptoms. For this spell you will need:

- An empty 10mls essential oil bottle with pipette.
- Bergamot essential oil.
- Cypress essential oil.
- Lemon essential oil.
- Cedarwood essential oil.
- Base oil.
- A white candle.

1. Make up the oil:

- X18 drops of Bergamot essential oil.
- X3 drops of Cypress essential oil.
- X6 drops of Lemon essential oil.

- X6 drops of Cedarwood essential oil.
- 5mls of Base oil.

2. Charge the oil and white candle with positive healing energy.

3. Light the candle and say these words:

Flame that flickers and flows,
Banish Depression woes,
Banish Anxiety before it grows.

Bring positivity bright,
Aid me now in this fight.
As I will it, so it is.

4. Allow candle to burn down fully.

5. Use the oil in baths by adding 10mls of milk to 1 pipette of the essential oils mix and release under the hot water tap.

Chakra Charm For Wellbeing

This is a charm for general wellbeing. For this charm you will need:

- A small charm bag.
- A small Carnelian to represent the Root Chakra.
- A small Sunstone to represent the Sacral Chakra.

- A small Citrine to represent the Solar Plexus Chakra.
- A small Aventurine to represent the Heart Chakra.
- A small Sodalite to represent the Throat Chakra.
- A small Amethyst to represent the Third Eye Chakra.
- A small Rose Quartz to represent the Spiritual/Higher Self Chakra.

Place crystals in charm bag, charge and carry on your person. If casting for someone else, have a photo of them and use this as a focus. Visualise them being in balance and harmony. Picture them in perfect health. Get them to carry on their person.

Headache Spritzer
Ease headaches with this headache spritzer. For this Spell you will need:

- An empty spritzer bottle.
- 50mls of boiled Water (allow to cool).
- Rosemary essential oil.
- Grapefruit essential oil.
- Peppermint essential oil.
- A small clear quartz crystal.

1. Boil water and allow to cool. Put water in empty spritzer bottle.

2. Place clear quartz crystal in the spritzer bottle.

3. Mix the following into the water and then give the spritzer a good shake:

- X9 drops of Rosemary essential oil.
- X14 drops of Grapefruit essential oil.
- X1 drop of Peppermint essential oil.

4. Shake and use when you have a headache for some instant relief.

Anti-Fatigue Bath

Fatigue is a terrible thing. We wanted to do something that was easy as we both know what it's like to feel drained and fatigued. So here's a simple bath remedy. For this bath remedy you will need:

- Rosemary essential oil.
- Vetiver essential oil.
- Lavender essential oil.
- 10mls of Milk.
- Amethyst crystal.

1. Mixed together:

- X11 drops of Rosemary essential oil.
- X6 drops of Vetiver essential oil.
- X10 drops of Lavender essential oil.

2. Then add the 10mls of milk and mix together.

3. Run a bath and release Anti-Fatigue Bath mixture under a hot tap.

4. Place an Amethyst crystal in the bath.

5. Have a relaxing bath. When it comes time to get out, stay in the bath and unplug it. As the water drains away, visualise your fatigue going with the water - down the drain.

6. Put the Amethyst crystal to one side and cleanse it as soon as you have the chance.

Take Away The Pain Spell
Does what it says in the title. For this spell you will need:

- A White teal light candle.
- A sharp nail.
- A stone.
- A small pot of paint or marker pen.

1. Mark the tea light on the top in the shape of a cross with the sharp nail saying:

Candle Light shine with health take away the pain

2. Hold the stone for a few seconds in the flame of the candle then rub the warm stone over the area causing

you pain saying:

Take the pain in natures stone,
free my body, free my bone.

3. After a few minutes take the paint or marker pen and write an X onto the stone. Then pour candle wax over the X and seal it in.

4. Take the stone as soon as you can to the nearest source of water and throw it in saying:

I cast away the pain as I cast away the stone.

A Charm & Spell for Good Teeth and Gums
If having dental problems please see a qualified Dentist. This Spell will help maintain good teeth and gums. For this spell you will need:

- A blue candle.
- Pink ribbon.
- Gold ribbon.
- Blue ribbon.
- A heart craft charm or symbol.
- Lavender herb.
- Clove herb.
- Myrrh essential oil.
- Lavender essential oil.
- Howlite crystal.
- A Charm bag.

1. Tie three knots in each of the ribbons saying as you do:

Knot one, the spell is begun,
Knot two, the spell goes on,
Knot three, the spell is done.

2. Place the ribbons in the charm bag along with the heart charm/heart symbol, some lavender and clove herbs. Next add the Howlite crystal.

3. Add to the bag 9 drops of Myrrh essential oil.

4. Charge with intention. If you are making this for someone else use a photo from when they had healthy teeth and gums as a focus, ensuring you choose a photo where they are smiling and genuinely happy. Your charm bag is now complete.

5. Close the bag and carry on your person or ask the person you are doing the spell for to carry on their person.

6. Charge the candle and anoint with lavender essential oil to seal the energy in. Light the candle over the next few nights, until it has burned all the way down.

To Ease Back Pain

Ease back pain with this Spell. For this spell you will need:

- Peppermint essential oil.
- Rosemary essential oil.
- Ginger essential oil.
- Lavender essential oil.
- Base oil.
- Someone willing to give you a back massage - alternatively you can release the oil mix under the hot tap and bathe in the oil.

1. Make up the massage oil:

- X1 drop of Peppermint essential oil.
- X4 drops of Rosemary essential oil.
- X9 drops of Ginger essential oil.
- X2 drops of Lavender essential oil.
- 10mls of Base oil.

2. The masseur should start in the place where the pain is and work outward. As he/she starts to massage he/she should say three times:

Back pain go away!
Leave [name]'s body today.
As my hands do ease the pain.
A painless back does [name] gain.

3. As the massage is coming to an end the masseur should say the above three times again.

Sleep Poppet

To aid a better night's sleep create yourself a sleep poppet. For this spell you will need:

- A poppet.
- Lavender flower.
- Lavender essential oil.
- Frankincense essential oil.
- Vetiver essential oil.

1. Make the poppet and fill with lavender flower.

2. Drop the following into the poppet before sealing it up:

- X3 drops of Lavender essential oil.
- X6 drops of Frankincense essential oil.
- X1 drop of Vetiver essential oil.

3. Take the poppet to bed with you for a good night's rest.

Sleep Tight Tonight Oil

The following recipe can be used by rubbing it into your temples or by burning in an oil burner half an hour before sleep. For this oil mix you will need:

- Chamomile essential oil.
- Star Anise essential oil.
- Geranium essential oil.
- Orange essential oil.
- Base oil.

Mix the following together:

- X4 drops of Chamomile essential oil.
- X4 drops of Star Anise essential oil.
- X9 drops of Geranium essential oil.
- X3 drops of Orange essential oil.
- 5mls of base oil.

To Evoke & Remember Your Dreams

Take an Amethyst crystal and a double-terminated clear quartz crystal. Place them under your pillow while you sleep. Be sure to have a notebook and pen at the side of your bed and write your dreams down in the night or morning when you wake. This is because you will only remember your dreams for a short time.

Meditation for Tranquility with Charm

For this meditation you will need:

- X1 White candle.
- X1 Smooth stone.
- Incense stick.
- Blue/white flowers.

1. Begin this meditation and charm on a Friday or after a very hectic day. Place the candle, stone, incense and flowers on a table where you can sit comfortably with both feet on the ground.

2. Light the candle and incense stick. Focus on the flame of the candle and take hold of the stone. Take a few deep breaths, inhale through your nose and exhale through your mouth. Continue this breathing while you let your mind become aware of the stone. Feel its weight and texture and let your awareness drop into the stone.

3. Let your inner vision recall a peaceful memory or landscape as you continue to hold the stone. Stay in this memory for as long as you wish.

4. When you have finished press the stone into the palm of your had to set the memory. Extinguish the candle and keep the stone with you.

5. Whenever you feel stressed hold the stone and press it into your palm. This will trigger the image of your

peaceful place and give you a feeling of calm.

6. You can always repeat the meditation to increase the power of the stone. This also works great if you substitute the stone for a crystal such as Blue Lace Agate, Aquamarine or Howlite.

Weight Loss
Eat less, move more. Padlock the fridge and hide the car keys.

Spots Be Gone Acne Face Wash
For this Face Wash you will need:

- Blue Chamomile essential oil.
- Niaouli essential oil.
- Tea Tree essential oil.
- Base oil.
- Milk.

1. Make up the oil mix:

- X1 drop of Blue Chamomile essential oil.
- X6 drops of Niaouli essential oil.
- X2 drops of Tea Tree essential oil.
- 10mls of Base oil.

2. Add x5 drops to 10mls of milk, then release under a hot

tap into a sink full of warm water. Wash with the water. Do this daily, once a day as a minimum, but ideally twice a day.

Triple Power Spots Be Gone
If you find that the Spots Be Gone Acne Face Wash isn't having the desired effect, it's time for more extreme measures. For this spell you will need:

- Blue Chamomile essential oil.
- Niaouli essential oil.
- Tea Tree essential oil.
- Base oil.
- An empty aromatherapy essential oils bottle with pipette.
- A Tee tree foaming face wash (available in most health and beauty shops or online).

1. Make up the Triple Power Spots Be Gone formula below and put into the empty essential oil bottle:

- X3 drop of Blue Chamomile essential oil.
- X18 drops of Niaouli essential oil.
- X6 drops of Tea Tree essential oil.
- 5mls of Base oil.

2. Twice daily, add 5 drops of the triple power formula to

a clean bowl of warm water. Rinse your skin with this water. Then wash using the tea tree foaming face wash, rinsing off in the same water. Your skin will feel cleansed. After say these words of power:

My skin is clear,
Beautiful I appear.
No blemishes or marks on my skin,
I am spot-free as I am within.

3. Results should start to show after 1 week of use.

Premenstrual Tension Bath Oil

Suffer with premenstrual tension? This bath oil will help and is best bathed in during a Waxing or Full Moon. For this you will need:
- Lavender essential oil.
- Sandalwood essential oil.
- Geranium essential oil.
- Ylang Ylang essential oil.
- Base oil.

1. Make up the oil using the following formula:
- X1 drop of Lavender essential oil.
- X5 drops of Sandalwood essential oil.
- X5 drops of Geranium essential oil.
- X3 drops of Ylang Ylang essential oil.
- 10mls Base oil.

2. Add 2-5 drops of the oil mix into your bath under the hot tap.

3. Get into the bath and relax. Try to imagine all the tension leaving your body and dispersing into the water.

Neptune Menopause Tea

For this spell you will need:

- A Citrine crystal.
- Spring water.
- Vodka.
- Chamomile Tea.

1. Place the Citrine crystal in 15mls of spring water for 24 hours. Next add 15mls of vodka. This is your Citrine Elixir. It should be stored in a dark cupboard and used within 28 days.

2. Make yourself a cup of Chamomile tea. Add to the tea 7 drops of your Citrine Elixir. As you drink the tea say:
I call on Neptune, from far away.
To help take the pains away.
No more flushes, for me today.
No more memory lapses.
Please hear what I say.

3. Repeat step 2 as required.

Health Correspondences

Colours	Crystals
• Blue • Purple • Red • Yellow • Orange • Light Green	• Rose Quartz • Clear Quartz • Moonstone • Tiger's Eye • Jasper • Bloodstone
Days of the Week	**Elements**
• Sunday • Monday • Tuesday	• Earth • Air
Essential Oils	**Phase(s) of The Moon**
• Carnation • Fennell • Lemon • Lime • Sandalwood • Cedarwood	• New Moon • Full Moon • Sunlight if possible.
Herbs, Trees & Plants	**Planets**
• Plants: Willow, Eucalyptus. • Trees: Willow, Apple Tree. • Herbs: Chamomile, Lavender, Sage.	• Earth • Sun

Love & Relationships

HANDFASTING

(The Marriage)

A marriage, a union, two separate hearts.

Drawn together here today never for to part.

Each heart brings its own foundations,

on which your love can build.

Each heart giving openly,

so both hearts are fulfilled.

Each heart stands sometimes alone,

but never out of reach.

Each heart must love and keep the home,

a tender safe retreat.

Let the winds blow round you both,

don't hold on too tight.

Give each other space to breathe,

and all will be alright.

Accept each other's differences.

Embrace each other's fears.

Face each challenge side by side,

and dry each other's tears.

Thank each other every day,

for always being there,

and even if your miles apart,

remember what you share.

For you have something special.

A love that shares a past.

A love, a beautiful future.

A love that's sure to last.

A Love Note

Love Spells are one of the oldest forms of magic. In this chapter you will find Spells to bring love into your life, to make you more open to the possibility of love and to strengthen existing relationships.

You won't find spells designed to get a specific person to fall in love with you. In our experience these sorts of spells often don't work and even when they do, the results are usually disastrous. With love magic the saying *be careful what you wish for* can't be understated.

With that in mind, on to the spells...

A Venus Love Spell

For this Spell you will need:

- A red candle.
- A candle holder.
- x2 sheets of red/pink paper cut into the shape of a heart.
- A small amount of your favourite perfume/after shave.
- A fire proof dish or fire proof cauldron.

1. Begin this Spell on a Friday, the day if Venus, the bringer of love. Create some quiet time for yourself, have a bath or shower and as you wash chant to yourself:

My body is beautiful, I am beautiful, I feel love, I attract love.

2. After your bath or shower light the red candle and think of all the positive qualities you would bring to a loving relationship. Write these on one of the paper hearts. Spray a little of your perfume/after shave on the heart, then carefully burn the heart in the fire proof dish or cauldron saying:

Venus take these words I write,
And lead me to a lover bright.

3. Next imagine all the attributes of an unknown person you wish to attract. Write these on the second paper heart and burn it in the candle flame saying:

Venus, find me a lover true,
Who matches these words I send to you.

4. Place the ashes in the fire proof dish or cauldron. Extinguish the candle.

5. Bury the ashes of the two hears outside your front door. Alternatively, if you live in a flat, bury them in a potted plant and place the plant as close to your front door as possible.

6. On the following nights continue to burn the candle for a few minutes each night and think of the words you sent to Venus.

7. When the candle is burned down to the last couple of inches bury it somewhere separate from where you buried the ashes. If you live in an apartment consider another potted plant.

8. Remember to look for signs of love over the next 28 days.

Love Powder Spell

This love powder is great for attracting a lover into your life. For this spell you will need:

- 2 teaspoons of Lavender Flower.
- 1 teaspoon of Ginger.
- 3 teaspoons of Cinnamon.
- 1/2 a teaspoon of Clove.

1. Mix herbs together.

2. Use in a charm bag to carry with you or sprinkle on a fire saying:

Flame burn and bring to me,
A lover who is all I need.
A partner for my future years.
Someone who will share my dreams.

Open Heart Spell

This Spell is good for anyone that has been hurt in the past and is ready to open their heart to love again. For this spell you will need:

- A red charm bag.
- A pink Agate or Red Tiger's Eye crystal.
- Jasmine essential oil.

- A red rose.

1. Stand in front of a mirror and chant three times:

My heart is an open door,
I ask for love and nothing more.
A partner to hold dear,
Someone close, whose always near.
Take away the pain of lovers past,
Bring to me a love to last.

2. Take the crystal and charge it with your intention. Next say:

Stone of love, stone of light,
My future lover shine so bright.

Let me notice him/her.
My walls kept down.
My heart open to love,
Do bless this spell spirits above.

Let a relationship develop and grow,
As I will it, stone make it so.

3. Anoint the crystal with Jasmine essential oil and place in the charm bag.

4. Gently take the red rose and remove the petals. Place the petals in the charm bag. Keep this charm bag with you until you meet someone special.

HandFasting Ritual

Lasting relationships are often symbolised by a commitment ceremony of some sort. Here is our version of a HandFasting, a pagan commitment ceremony.

1. Stand the couple in the circle one facing south and one facing north.

2. Cast the circle saying:

We draw this circle as a token,
Eternal love that is never broken.
It has no end there is no start,
And symbolises two open hearts.

3. The couple are led to the centre of the circle where they join hands.

4. Take the rings and a red ribbon or rope to each of the quarters and say.

Guardians of the East bringer of Air empower these rings with your energies giving the qualities or Air. Space and freedom, communication and creativity.

Guardians of the South bringer of Fire empower these rings with your energies giving the qualities of Fire. Passion and love, power and energy

Guardians of the West bringer of Water empower these rings with your energies giving the qualities of Water. Deep understanding, dreams and compassion.

Guardians of the North bringer of Earth empower these rings with your energies giving the qualities of Earth.

Security and stability, foundations and growth.

With the Elements around us we celebrate the joining of
_____ *&* _____ *who have come together willingly*
with perfect love and perfect trust.

5. The rings are exchanged and the couple say their heart song* to each other.

6. Then take the red ribbon or rope and bind the couple's hands together saying:

The elements have combined to create this sacred space.
Let the Moon shine down on this union and this place.
May you live and laugh together until the stars grow cold.

7. Bless the cakes and ale and feast.

8. The guests can bestow gifts at this point.

9. Then a doorway is opened in the East the guests line up on either side of the doorway and the couple walk along the passage made by the guests as the guests throw rose petals over the couple.

10. Once the couple have left the circle say:

As _____ *&* _____ *set out on a new adventure*
the circle is open but not broken. Merry meet, merry part
and merry meet again.

* A heart song is either spoken vows to one another or vows that are sung to one another.

Love Correspondences

Colours	Crystals
• Red • Pink	• Pink Agate • Ruby • Moonstone • Pink Carnelian • Pink Tourmaline • Red Tiger's Eye
Days of the Week	**Elements**
• Friday • Thursday	• Fire • Water
Essential Oils	**Phase(s) of The Moon**
• Lime • Lavender • Jasmine • Ginger • Apricot	• New Moon • Full Moon
Herbs, Trees & Plants	**Planets**
• Plants: Rose, Daffodil & Apple Blossom. • Trees: Apple, Willow & Apricot. • Herbs: Basil, Geranium, Saffron, Marjoram.	• Venus • Moon

Luck

A GLIMMER OF HOPE

A silver dollar, a rabbit's tail, a horse shoe or a clover.

I'm searching for a helping hand to get this bad spell over.

I only need a glimmer of hope to make the world feel right.

I only need a stroke of luck to get me through the night.

I can't believe I got so low searching for the truth.

I understand that time will change I've known it from my youth.

I really need a helping hand to get this bad spell over.

Yet still I stand with flowers in hand and 3 leaves on my clover.

Lucky, Lucky, Lucky: A Short Note on Luck Magic

Luck magic is an interesting area of magic. For what is luck? How does it manifest? One thing we know about luck is that it is very subjective. What some may consider luck, others would consider misfortune. A good way to work luck magic is to practice gratitude. Whatever your views on luck, the tried and tested spells in this chapter will bring more luck into your life. Things will start to go your way. With that written, on to the spells...

Your Lucky Charm

This charm is perfect for attracting luck into your life. For this spell you will need:

- A gold charm bag.
- Star Anise essential oil.
- Vetiver essential oil.
- Orange essential oil.
- Base oil.
- X7 dried rose petals.
- X7 hazel leaves.
- Nutmeg.
- A Sunstone crystal.

1. Make up The Fantastic Luck Oil:

- X5 drops of Star Anise essential oil.
- X3 drops of Vetiver essential oil.
- X8 drops of Orange essential oil.
- 5mls of Base oil.

2. Put the oil to one side.

3. Make up the charm bag by adding to the bag:

- X7 dried rose petals.
- X7 hazel leaves.
- 1/2 a teaspoon of Nutmeg.
- X1 Sunstone crystal.
- X3 drops of The Fantastic Luck Oil.

4. Each day you will 'feed' the bag a drop of The Fantastic Luck Oil and as you do this say:

I add life to this charm,
Bring forth luck without any harm.

Lucky Note Spell
This luck Spell involves money. For this spell you will need:

- Star Anise essential oil.
- Vetiver essential oil.
- Orange essential oil.
- A marker pen (ideally green, but not essential).
- A £5, $5 note/bill of your currency.

1. Make up The Fantastic Luck Oil:

- X5 drops of Star Anise.

- X3 drops of Vetiver.
- X8 drops of Orange.
- 5mls of Base oil.

2. Draw the symbol of Jupiter on the £5/$5 note using the marker pen. It looks like this:

3. Anoint the notes with The Fantastic Luck Oil and carry around in your purse/wallet. Just be sure not to spend the note or you'll be passing your good fortune on to another.

Lady Luck Spell
For this spell you will need:

- A gold candle.
- Star Anise essential oil.

1. Charge and intent the candle. Anoint with Star Anise.

2. Light the candle and say:

I am as lucky as can be,
Lady Luck smile down on me.

Make me lucky in all I do.
Everything working out just as I want it to.

Nothing can go wrong for me now,
I succeed in all endeavors somehow.

Each day that passes the magic grows,
The power of luck flows.

I am lucky now and always.
So mote it be.

3. Allow the candle to burn down fully to release the energy into the cosmos.

A Spell for Business/Workplace Luck

For this spell you will need:

- Green paper and a pen.
- A green charm bag.
- A bloodstone crystal.
- X3 coins of your currency.

1. Using the paper and pen draw the following rune:

2. Put the piece of paper with the drawn rune on into the charm bag, along with the bloodstone and x3 coins.

3. Charge the bag in sunlight for 7 days then carry around with you at work or your place of business to attract luck.

The 5,4,3,2,1 Luck For Others Box
This Spell is ideal for bringing luck into another person's life. For this spell you will need:

- A small wooden box, the type you can pick up in craft shops cheaply.
- Fingernail/toenail clippings or hair from the person you want to cast the spell on.
- Dried rose petals.
- X1 Tiger's Eye crystal.
- 1/2 a teaspoon of Nutmeg.
- Orange essential oil.
- Lemon essential oil.

- Star Anise essential oil.
- Ginger essential oil.
- Vetiver essential oil.
- A marker pen.

1. Add the following to the box:

- Some dried rose petals.
- X1 Tiger's Eye crystal.
- 1/2 a teaspoon of Nutmeg.
- X5 drops of Orange essential oil.
- X4 drops of Lemon essential oil.
- X3 drops of Star Anise essential oil.
- X2 drops of Ginger essential oil.
- X1 Drop of Vetiver essential oil.

2. Close the box and give it a good shake.

3. Write the name of the person who wish to bring luck to on the box. Also draw the following rune on the box:

4. Decorate the box nicely so that it can be given as a gift to the person you want to bring good luck to.

5. When you give the box to the person you want to bring luck to, tell them to add anything that makes them feel lucky into the box. This could be symbols drawn on paper, a bit of material off lucky clothes, etc.

Luck Correspondences

Colours	Crystals
• Blue • Silver • Gold • Yellow • Orange	• Tiger's Eye • Rutilated Quartz • Apache Tear • Silver Ore • Bloodstone • Jade • Sunstone
Days of the Week • Thursday • Sunday	**Elements** • Air • Earth
Essential Oils • Vetiver • Orange • Star Anise • Nutmeg • Rose	**Phase(s) of The Moon** • New Moon • Full Moon • Even better if you can work in sunlight.
Herbs, Trees & Plants • Plants: Bluebell, Daffodil, Heather. • Trees: Oak, Holly, Hazel. • Herbs: All Spice, Nutmeg, Poppyseed, Clover.	**Planets** • Jupiter

Protection

PURPLE, BLUE & BLACK

Ribbons of Purple, Blue & Black,

Keep me shielded from any attack.

As I knot the ribbons together,

Keep me safe forever.

I knot once, I knot twice,

I knot three times, thrice.

For three is the magic number.

I am protected. By this charm.

Let me never come to harm.

A Witch Bottle for Self-Protection

Witch bottles have been used for protection for centuries. For this Witch's bottle you will need:

- A small bottle with cork lid.
- Hair and/or finger/toe nail clippings.
- X3 drawing pins.
- X3 nails.
- X3 small pieces of Haematite.
- X3 small pieces of Clear Quartz.
- X3 small pieces of Amethyst.
- X3 small pieces of Lapis Lazuli.
- A purple candle.
- Lime essential oil.
- Patchouli essential oil.
- Star Anise essential oil.
- Some Vodka.

1. Place the hair and/or finger/toe nails in the small bottle, followed by the drawing pins and nails.

2. Next place the crystals in the bottle.

3. Charge the candle with the visualisation of you being surround by an impenetrable purple bubble that lets positive energy come and go, but blocks out all negative energy. Remember when doing this that everything is energy on some frequency vibration or another.

4. Add to the bottle:

- X3 drops of Lime essential oil.
- X3 drops of Patchouli essential oil.
- X3 drops of Star Anise essential oil.

5. Add some Vodka to the bottle. Alcohol kills all bacteria and this is the reason for adding this final ingredient. We added x3 caps full off a miniature bottle of vodka.

6. Light the candle and seal the bottle with wax.

7. Then you can either bury the bottle or candle or both on your property, or if you live in an apartment put the bottle facing the door. You can also burn the candle whenever you feel that you need extra protection.

Protection Knot Spell & Charm
For this Spell you will need:

- X1 White Candle.
- Red thread.
- Gold thread.
- Green thread.

1. Carve your name into the white candle.

2. Light the candle saying:

Circle of light keep me safe,
Guard me well and banish my fears.

3. Take the red thread and imagine yourself in a circle of red light. Tie three knots into the red thread saying:

Red light of fire circle and protect me.

4. Take the gold thread and imagine a golden light shining down over you. Tie three knots into the gold thread saying:

Golden light of air, shine down and protect me.

5. Take the green thread and imagine green earth energy rising up into your body. Tie three knots into the green thread saying:

Green light of earth support and protect me.

6. Finally plait the three threads together by knotting one end first and then plaiting down the length of the thread. Dip the untied end of the threads into the melted wax of the candle to seal them saying:

White light of water bind this charm and protect me.

7. Wear or carry the plaited braid with you as a charm.

ABC (Anise, Basil & Carnelian) Charm for the Protection of Others

Want to provide others with protection? Then use this charm. For this spell you will need:

- Paper and a pen.
- A purple charm bag.
- Peppercorns.
- Basil (herb).
- A Carnelian crystal.
- Star Anise essential oil.
- Myrrh essential oil.
- Sandalwood essential oil.

1. Draw the following rune on the piece of paper:

2. Place the paper in the charm bag. Feel free to cut the paper down to a size that will easily fit in the charm bag.

3. Next add the following to the charm bag:

- 7 Peppercorns (one for each day of the week).
- X3 drops of Star Anise essential oil,
- 1/2 a teaspoon of Basil.
- X1 Carnelian crystal,
- X6 drops of Myrrh essential oil.
- X6 drops of Sandalwood essential oil.

Please note: The charm bag will smell very rich, this is intentional, as we wanted it to smell so good that one would not forget to carry it on their person.

3. Close the charm bag.

4. Say these words of power over the charm bag and at the end of each line draw the rune for protection (above) over the charm bag with your wand or athame:

By the Powers of the Moon and Stars,
I call upon the Power of the Planet Mars.
Protect [name] whatever he/she shall do,
Wherever he/she shall travel through.
Keep them safe at all times.
Protect them with this runic sign.

Incantation for the Protection of Others

1. Say this incantation to protect another:

Powers of the Earth,
Protect [name] from birth.
No harm shall come to thee,
A protective green bubble be.

Powers of the air,
Protect [name] everywhere.
No harm shall come to thee,
A protective yellow shield be.

Powers of Water and tide,
Protect [name]'s every stride.
No harm shall come to thee,
A protective blue bubble be.

Powers of Fire and flame,
Protect [name] I exclaim!
No harm shall come to thee,
A protective red shield be.

Protected by the elements you are,
Safe you be near or afar.
So mote it be.

Home Protection: A Crystal Grid

A crystal grid is a combination of crystals that are joined together for a shared purpose. The grid usually has one central crystal. Antony uses a large clear quartz cluster for his home protection grid and Luna uses an Amethyst geode arch for his. Start by getting together appropriate crystals for the grid.

They don't all have to be the same type of crystal; in fact many Magical Practitioners uses different crystals for different purposes. For example, Antony uses Smokey Quartz crystals over his bathroom doors for Smokey Quartz's properties of dispelling negativity. Yet uses Amethyst for his front door and windows for Amethyst's protective qualities.

Cleanse and charge your crystals. You should place your smaller crystals on or around your central crystal as they charge. Then going clockwise around your house, place the crystals where you want them. Good places include over doorways, windows, in corners of rooms, etc. If using crystals with a point try and place the point outward or upward if possible.

Once all the crystals are in place, take your wand or athame starting at your central crystal and tap it gently. Then visualising energy coming from the central crystal follow you to the first crystal in your grid. Tap the crystal gently and see the connection between the two formed.

Do this for all of the crystals. Go back to the central crystal, charge it with your intention. Feel it pass this task through vibrations to the other crystals in the grid. Feel the grid go from two dimensional to three dimensional. There you have your home protection crystal grid.

One thing to note when charging your intention: you want to keep the negative out, but allow the positive in. Don't forget about the positive and block all energy from entering your home. If you do that, not only will you no longer have any visitors (this might be a plus!), but it stops anything good you do from entering your house as well.

A crystal grid will last a long time, especially if you intent the main crystal to draw its power from the universe and to recharge the other crystals in the grid. Doing that will make the protection timeless, always present. But should circumstances change you can always break and disassemble the crystal grid by doing the opposite of what you did to create it.

Charm For Travel Protection

If you are traveling, carry the following charm on your person for safe travels. This can also be adapted to provide travel protection for others. For this spell you will need:

- Blue charm bag.
- Clove of garlic.
- Rock salt.
- A piece of paper with the rune for travel.
- An Amethyst crystal.

1. Place the Amethyst crystal, the piece of paper with the Rune for travel (below) and the garlic in the charm bag. The rune for safe travel is:

2. Cover the contents of the bag with salt. Then close the charm bag.

3. Chant these words six times over the charm bag:

Travel safe near and far,
All be well wherever you are.
As I will it, so more it be.

Magic Square Talisman for Protection of Children

For this Talisman you will need:

- Jupiter Magic Square. (Shown below)
- Blue or purple pen/ marker.
- Purple thread.
- Needle.
- Piece of blue felt approximately 10cm x 10cm.
- A purple charm bag.

Jupiter Magic Square

04. 14. 15. 01

09. 07. 06. 12

05. 11. 10. 08

16. 02. 03. 13

1. Reduce the child's name to numbers where 1 = A and so on, for example:

R Y. A. N = 18. 25. 1. 14

2. The Jupiter square only has numbers up to 16 so continue to reduce the numbers by adding them together so

R = 18. = 9.

Y = 25 = 7

A = 1

N = 14

3. Place a thin piece of paper over the magic square and trace a line from the first number to the second and so on until you have done the whole name.

4. Transfer the sigil (shape) to the felt and then stitch over the mark with the thread concentrating on the child and asking for protection.

5. Place the felt in the charm bag and charge it on a window sill overnight then if possible, let the child carry it with them. A good way for a child to carry the talisman is by placing it in a Perspex key ring.

Pets Protection Spell

Pets are part of the family for most people, so here's a way to protect your fury friends. For this spell you will need:

- X1 purple candle.
- Lavender essential oil.
- Vetiver essential oil.

1. On a Full Moon cast a circle. Take the purple candle

and charge it with this chant:

Zeus and Hera I conjure thee,
Come forth and help me.
Lend your Powers to this spell,
Keep my pets fit and well.

Protect them from any harm,
As I chant this magic charm.

Let their lives be full and good.
Let these words be understood.

So it is and so shall it be.

2. When you are satisfied that the candle is charged with your intention, anoint the candle with Lavender and the wick with Vetiver.

3. Light the candle and allow it to burn down fully.

Powerful Protection Incense
This incense offers powerful protection. For this incense you will need:

- Frankincense Resin.
- Valerian Root.
- Sage (herb).
- Rose petals (preferably dried).
- Willow Bark.

- Cinnamon Powder.
- Juniper essential oil.
- Vetiver essential oil.
- Patchouli essential oil.
- Lime essential oil.

1. Make the incense by grinding together the following in a mortar and pestle:

- X1 Tablespoon of Frankincense Resin.
- X1 Teaspoon of Valerian Root.
- A pinch of Sage (herb).
- X1 Tablespoon of Rose petals (preferably dried).
- X1 Teaspoon of Willow Bark.
- 1/2 Teaspoon of Cinnamon Powder.
- X10 drops of Juniper essential oil.
- X10 drops of Vetiver essential oil.
- X5 drops of Patchouli essential oil.
- X10 drops of Lime essential oil.

2. Burn this incense throughout your home with the doors and windows open. Leaving the doors and windows open allows negative energy to leave.

Protection Correspondences

Colours	Crystals
• Purple • Black • Dark Blue	• Danburite • Amethyst • Blue Lace Agate • Chrysoberyl • Bloodstone • Carnelian
Days of the Week	**Elements**
• Sunday • Monday • Thursday	• Fire • Earth
Oils & Incense	**Phase(s) of The Moon**
• Star Anise • Frankincense • Bergamot • Cypress • Myrrh • Sandalwood	• Full Moon • New Moon • Even better if you can work in sunlight.
Herbs, Trees & Plants	**Planets**
• Plants: Anise, Mistletoe, Honeysuckle, Rose and Marigold. • Trees: Pine. • Herbs: Sage.	• Sun • Moon

Transformative

PAN DANCE

Dance on cushions of needles,

Neath the branches of Pine and Yew.

Take your warmth from the fire in the clearing,

As you circle the flames and jump through.

Call to Pan as the passion increases,

As he steps from the trees out to dance,

And listen to drums and the pipes of the Lord.

As your senses fall into a trance,

Feel free as your face hits the cold air,

See the face of the man in the trees.

Listen to all that he tells you.

Euphoria drags you to your knees,

Lie exhausted and spent in the moonlight.

Catch your breath on the cold of the night.

Feel the gift of the Gods deep inside you,

Don't resist cause there's no need to fight.

Be at one with the Earth and the Sky up above.

As the land receives warmth from the Sun,

When the first ray of sunshine falls onto your face,

Give thanks for the gatherings done.

To Be Noticed By All

Feeling like nobody knows that you're around? Or that you haven't had your perfect moment to shine? Then this Spell is perfect for you. For this Spell you will need:

- Grapefruit essential oil.
- Ginger essential oil.
- Green and Gold wire.
- Gold glitter.
- A small mirror.
- A small star.
- X2 googly eyes.
- A yellow candle.
- A orange candle.
- A charm bag.

1. Take the gold and green wire and intertwine it into a spiral shape. Place it in the bag visualising you at the centre of everyone's attention.

2. Add to the bag some gold glitter, the small mirror, the small star and googly eyes. As you do, visualise all eyes on you and see yourself being recognised by those you wish would see you.

3. Charge and give your intention to the candles.

4. Drip into the charm bag x6 drops of each candle, then extinguish.

5. Add 9 drops of Grapefruit essential oil and 3 drops of Ginger essential oil into the bag.

6. Now go to a mirror and recite the following three times to yourself:

Bring the spotlight.
Now is the time.
Recognise my time to shine.
By Mercury's gift & Jupiter's might,
I Be Noticed on this night.

7. Carry the charm bag with you.

8. For each of the next two nights burn down the two candles, one a night.

To Hide An Object (in Plain Sight)
Use this chant to hide an object in plain sight. As you chant the words visualise the object going invisible and people ignoring it. Chant this at least 9 times over the object:

No one will see you.
No one will care.
No one will touch you.
No one will dare.
You'll be ignored by all but me.
So mote it be.

This Spell can also be adapted to hide people and places, but should be used with caution in these cases.

A Charm for Courage

Need to be more courageous? To face your fears and do it anyway? Then this Spell is for you. For this spell you will need:

- A red charm bag.
- X1 Unakite crystal.
- X4 Malachite crystals.
- A dragon charm or charm that represents courage to you.
- X16 Cracked black pepper corns.
- Red felt.
- A marker pen.
- A teaspoon of Lavender seed.

1. Take the charm bag and place the following in it: x1 Unakite crystal, x4 Malachite crystals, the dragon charm and the x16 cracked black pepper corns.

2. Cut the red felt to the size of the charm bag and draw the rune for courage on it using the marker pen. The rune for courage looks like this:

3. Put the felt and a teaspoon of Lavender seed into the charm bag. Then close.

4. Chant the following four times over the charm bag:

Lilith give me courage to overcome my fears,
Give me power to fight, Lilith won't you hear.
Charge this charm with all your might let the power grow,
Lilith come to my aid won't you help me so.

5. Carry on your person whenever you feel the need for additional courage.

Inspiration Bath Oil
Needing a little inspiration in your life? Then drop 2-5 drops of this formula into the bath, relax and let your mind be inspired with ideas:

- X5 drops of Sandalwood essential oil.

- X3 drops of Orange essential oil.
- X1 drop of Rosemary essential oil.

It might be worth keeping a notebook and pen close by to jot your ideas down after the bath.

Creativity Candle Spell

This Spell is perfect for those what start creative projects but never seem to finish them. For this spell you will need:

- X1 Yellow Candle.
- Lemon essential oil.
- An Amethyst point.

1. Charge the candle with your intention.

2. Mark the candle with the symbol for Uranus. The symbol for Uranus looks like this:

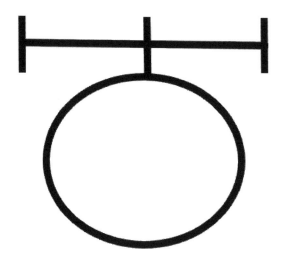

3. Anoint the candle with the Lemon essential oil.

4. Light the candle and say three times:
Athena and the Muses come to me,
Hear my creative plea.
Uranus, we'll have you as well,
Make my creative juices swell.

Make me productive, my projects grow,
Inspire me with the things that you know.

Let me complete my great work soon,
By the powers of Uranus and the moon.

So mote it be.

5. Charge the Amethyst point with your intention. Place it next to the lit candle until the candle has burned all the way down. Then carry the Amethyst point with you and keep it in your line of sight when working on your

creative projects.

Cloud-Bursting
To clear the clouds from the sky.

1. Focus on a large cloud and visualise the wind blowing through the thickest part of the cloud and say:

Four winds blow and clear the sky,
Wave these heavy clouds goodbye.
Let the Sun show his face,
Bless me with his warm embrace.

To Ask For Rain
Does what it says in the title.

1. Take a bowl of water outside place your hand in the bowl and say:

Mother earth release your tears,
Bless us with a fruitful year.
Rain down on this garden green,
A shower to keep air fresh and clean.

2. Raise your hand from the water and sprinkle it over the ground and say:

I bless you and thank you.

Holiday: Good Weather Spell

For this spell you will need

- A calendar.
- A yellow marker.
- A Sunstone.

1. Mark a sun symbol on a calendar with a yellow marker the days you are going away and write the outdoor activities you wish to do while you are away.

Hold the Sunstone and say:

Bless me with a week of sun,
Bless me with a week of fun.
Let the time we are away,
Be filled with sunshine every day.

2. Place the sunstone on a window sill in direct sunlight and repeat the mantra until you go on holiday then take the Sunstone with you.

Empowerment Talisman

For this talisman you will need:

- A piece of Oak wood (for men) or a piece Holly wood (for women).
- Some Gold or Red wire.
- A Pyrography kit.

1. Mark your name in Ogham script on the wood vertically using your Pyrography kit. The Ogham script

can be easily found online. For example, SAM would be:

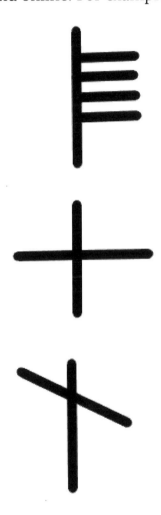

2. Wrap the gold or red wire around the wood.

3. Then you can either:

- Make it into a wand or,
- Wear it as a piece of jewelry or,
- Hang it in your home.

WishCraft

MAKE A WISH

Blow out a candle and make a wish.

It's one of the oldest spells,

As is throwing coins into wells.

Magic is: Wonderful. A miracle. Prayers answered.

Weave your magic,

The results will never be tragic.

The results will be beyond what you could imagine.

Wish Cord Spell

Have a wish you'd love to see fulfilled? Use this wish Spell. For this spell you will need:

- A white cord or cord coloured to Correspond with your wish.
- Incense.

1. Pass the cord through incense to cleanse it.

2. Next knot the cord as you say the following (one knot for each line):

As I tie knot one, the spells begun.
As I tie two, the wish is true.
As I tie three, my will is free.
As I tie four, the wish will soar.
As I tie five, the spells alive.
As I tie six, the wish we fix.
As I tie seven, the wish is given.
As I tie eight, we now must wait.
As I tie nine, it comes in time.

The Tree Wish Spell

This spell involves getting out in nature. It is great for Spells for long term goals or for long lasting effects. For this spell you will need:

- A ribbon in the colour that corresponds with your wish.
- A marker pen.

- An essential oil that corresponds with your wish.
- Water in a bottle.

1. Take the ribbon and marker pen. Write a short phrase that represents your wish on the ribbon. If possible come up with a phrase that rhymes.

2. Knot either end of the ribbon saying your phrase and imaging your wish come true.

3. Anoint the ribbon with three drops of essential oil on each knot while repeating your phrase three times.

4. Go out in nature and find a tree that corresponds with your wish. Tie your ribbon onto the branch of the tree.

5. Give the tree a gift of water from your bottle as a token of thanks.

Note: An alternative variation of this spell is throwing a coin in a wishing well. This simple act can be a powerful spell, just remember to take a couple of minutes to charge your coin with your intention before throwing it into the water. Fresh running water is most effective for this spell. Steer clear of wishing wells that are intended to make their owners money.

Good Day Bath
Bathe in a few drops of the following oil mix in the morning to guarantee a good day. For this spell you will need:

- Cypress essential oil.
- Juniper essential oil.
- Lime essential oil.
- Lemon essential oil.
- Orange essential oil.
- Base oil.

1. Make up the oil mix:

- X4 drops of Cypress essential oil.
- X4 drops of Juniper essential oil.
- X2 drops of Lime essential oil.
- X4 drops of Lemon essential oil.
- X4 drops of Orange essential oil.
- 5mls base oil.

2. Add 2-5 drops into the bath, under the hot tap.

I Don't Wanna Do It
This spell is for occasions where you have committed to do something that you'd rather not do. For this spell you will need:

- X1 black candle.
- Patchouli essential oil.

This spell should be cast on a Sunday when you have something the following week that you've committed too but don't really want to do.

1. Scratch on the candle the date of the event that you wish to miss.

2. Anoint the candle with Patchouli.

3. Charge the candle by saying three times:

Lord and Lady grant my wish.
This engagement I'd like to miss.
See to it now that something crops up.
That suits both parties and looks like luck.

Balance Spritzer
To bring your life into a more balanced state make up this spritzer and spray around your home. For this spell you will need:

- Empty spritzer bottle.
- Rose water.
- Water.
- Star Anise essential oil.
- Ylang Ylang essential oil.
- Spearmint essential oil.
- Yellow food colouring.

1. Make up the spritzer bottle:

- 20mls Rose water.

- 40mls water.
- 5 drops of Star Anise essential oil.
- 5 drops of Ylang Ylang essential oil.
- 2 drops of Spearmint essential oil.
- 2 drops of yellow food colouring.

2. Spray whenever you feel unbalanced.

The Marvelous Magical Boosting Incense
For this incense you will need:

- Frankincense resin.
- Mugwort dried herb.
- Yarrow Bark.
- Bay Leaves.
- Star Anise dried herb.
- Calendula dried herb.
- Ground Nutmeg.
- Cinnamon powder.
- Orange essential oil.
- Lemon essential oil.

1. Make up the incense by grinding together the following using a pestle and mortar:

- X1 Tablespoon of Frankincense resin.
- X1 Teaspoon of Mugwort.
- X1 Teaspoon of Yarrow Bark.
- X1 large Bay leaf.

- X1 Teaspoon of Calendula.
- 1/2 a Teaspoon of ground Nutmeg.
- 1/4 a Teaspoon of Cinnamon powder.
- X10 drops of Orange essential oil.
- X10 drops of Lemon essential oil.

2. Burn during spellcraft or ritual on a piece of charcoal.

Reduce & Eliminate Fear Charm Bag

Fear can freeze us in our tracks. It can hold us back and stop us reaching our full potential. To reduce or eliminate fear use this Spell. For this spell you will need:

- X1 Black charm bag.
- A marker pen.
- X1 Black Onyx crystal.
- Hibiscus flowers (dried) or rose petals (dried).
- Yarrow Bark.
- Rosemary (herb.)
- Ginger essential oil.
- Sandalwood essential oil.
- Juniper essential oil.
- Ylang Ylang essential oil.
- An empty essential oils bottle, ideally with pipette.

1. Cleanse and charge the Black Onyx crystal in the usual way. Give your crystal its intention by visualising the crystal absorbing fear and transforming it into neutral energy. Then visualise the neutral energy being returned

to you.

2. Draw the Thorn rune symbol on the bay leaf using the marker pen. The Thorn rune looks like this:

3. Make up the charm bag:

- X1 teaspoon of Hibiscus flowers (dried) or rose petals (dried).

- X1 teaspoon of Yarrow Bark.
- X1 teaspoon of Rosemary (herb).
- X1 drop of Ginger essential oil.
- X3 drops of Sandalwood essential oil.
- X3 drops of Juniper essential oil.
- X2 drops of Ylang Ylang essential oil.

4. Make up the oil as below and put it into the empty essential oils bottle:

- 5mls of base oil.

- X1 drop of Ginger essential oil.
- X3 drops of Sandalwood essential oil.
- X3 drops of Juniper essential oil.
- X2 drops of Ylang Ylang essential oil.

5. Each day 'feed' your charm bag a drop of the oil and say:

Mighty Jupiter take my fear,
Focus my thoughts and keep them clear.
Accept this offering every day,
Fear be gone! Go away.

6. Carry the charm bag with you, particularly when going into situations that make you feel fearful. The oil can also be worn as a perfume or aftershave.

Find A Home
Need to find your ideal home? Then this creative Spell is for you. For this spell you need:
- An A3 piece of yellow card.
- Various home magazines/catalogues.
- Scissors.
- Glue.
- Wallpaper samples and/or Fabric samples.
- Coloured pens.

1. You are going to create a vision board of your ideal home. First take the A3 card and visualise every aspect of your ideal home.

2. Out of the magazines/catalogues cut out images of things you would like in your home. Stick these to your card.

3. Write key words in the colour scheme you would like your new home to have on the card. For example: comfort, warm, good school nearby, 3 bedrooms, room for pets, etc.

4. Add wallpaper samples or fabric samples to your card.

5. Add appropriate symbols to your card. We would highly recommend that you add the symbol for Hestia, goddess of home and hearth. Her symbol looks like this:

6.Place the card on an East wall, somewhere that you will see it every day.

7. Add to the vision board as you find more images, samples and symbols.

8. Spend at least 5 minutes per day looking at your vision board and visualising every aspect of living in your new home.

Sell A House

For this spell you will need:
- A deck of Tarot Cards.
- Tracing Paper.
- A Pencil.
- Gold Paper.
- A Marker pen.
- A Gold Charm Bag.
- Your Estate Agents Business Card.
- Rose petals (dried).
- Frankincense essential oil.
- Myrrh essential oil.
- Cinnamon essential oil.
- Sandalwood essential oil.

1. Stuff the gold charm bag with rose petals (dried) and add in your Estate Agents Business Card. Then add the following essential oils:
- X3 drops of Frankincense essential oil.
- X6 drops of Myrrh essential oil.
- X1 drop of Cinnamon essential oil.
- X3 drops of Sandalwood essential oil.

2. Seal the charm bag and hang over the front door.

3. Using the marker pen draw the symbol for Hestia on the back of your For Sale sign. The symbol for Hestia looks like this:

4. Take the Four of Wands out of your Tarot Deck and trace it on to the centre of the gold paper. Next add symbols around the Tarot card tracing. For example: you might add a currency symbol, or draw signed contracts, or even a champagne bottle. Place this in your window, facing the sunrise direction if possible.

5. Finally, more a tip than magic. If possible, bake fresh bread before a viewing, as it will welcome viewers and make them more comfortable.

A List of Awesome Books

Here is a biography of awesome books. We have only listed books that are still in print (at time of publishing SpellCast) and are therefore available to buy:

- A Witch Alone by Marien Green (2002)

- Advanced Witchcraft by Edain McCoy (2004)

- Druid Magic by Maya Sutton & Nicholas Mann (2000)

- Elements of Witchcraft by Ellen Dugan (2003)

- Everyday Magic by Dorothy Morrison (1998)

- Natural Magic by Doreen Valiente (1999)

- The Complete Book of Incense, Oils & Brews by Scott Cunningham (1989)

- The Crystal Bible by Judy Hall (2003)

- The Crystal Bible Volume 2 by Judy Hall (2009)

- The Witch's Bag of Tricks by Melanie Marquis (2011)

- Utterly Wicked Curses, Hexes & Other Unsavory Notions by Dorothy Morrison (2007)

- Witchcraft Theory and Practice by Ly De Angeles (2000)

Index

Acknowledgements

Luna Hare would like to thank the following:

Janet and Jim Hilton, Martin Fairhurst, Stuart Bewley and Antony Simpson for their continuing support and friendship. Also Joan and Alf Withington and Chrys Ritson for their Magic and their inspiration. Finally, I would like to thank all the many people I have shared a Magic Circle with. Bright Blessings to you all.

Antony Simpson would like to thank the following:

Sarah Croney (mum),all of my family and the Watts Family for their love and support. Also to each and every reader that had bought a copy of this book – thank you! I can't wait to hear your thoughts. Brightest blessings to you all.

Printed in Great Britain
by Amazon